Ash Glazes

For Lynne and Claire

Ash Glazes

Phil Rogers

A&C Black • London
Chilton Book Company • Radnor, Pennsylvania

First published in Great Britain 1991
A & C Black (Publishers) Limited
35 Bedford Row, London WC1R 4JH

ISBN 0–7136–3440–5

A CIP catalogue record for this book is available from
the British Library

First published in USA by Chilton Book Company, Radnor,
Pennsylvania 19089.

ISBN 0–8019–8243–X

Jacket illustrations

front: pot by Author

back: detail of pot by Author

Designed by Janet Watson.

Photographs by Bill Thomas.

Frontispiece   A squared and incised bottle, 13" tall.
This bottle was thrown in one piece but before the neck was
collared over the body it was pushed out with a finger to
suggest four corners. Later, at the leather hard stage, the body
of the pot was beaten with a wooden panel to emphasise the
'squareness'. The incised marks were made with the corner of a
hacksaw blade. It has a straw ash glaze and a walnut ash glaze
over the neck. Reduction fired 1280°C.

Filmset by Latimer Trend & Company Ltd, Plymouth
Printed in Hong Kong by Wing King Tong Co., Ltd.

Contents

Acknowledgements

I should like to extend my sincere thanks to a number of people without whose help this book would not have been possible.

Firstly, to Bill Thomas for his magnificent colour photography, for his endless patience and infinite care. Secondly, to the potters who gave up their valuable time to talk to me and to those who supplied me with photographs of their work or pots to photograph, especially Tom Turner and his photographer Ken Van Dyne. To the various museums that have made material available and particularly to Dr Impey and Mary Tregear of the Ashmolean in Oxford for their help. Also to Bonhams and Christies, and Manson & Woods Ltd. for photographic material.

To Nigel Wood, who kindly read and corrected the manuscript for the historical section and Lance Mytton at the Welsh Plant Breeding Station for his advice and help with the botanical section and for supplying many of the analyses. To Moira Vincintelli and the University of Wales Collection for permission to photograph Katherine Pleydell-Bouverie's work. To Gas Kimishima for allowing me to photograph his collection and for doing some investigative work on my behalf in Japan. To Laser Kilns Ltd. of North London for generously supplying one of their kilns in which to carry out glaze tests.

There were also a number of people who responded kindly to an enquiring phone call, probably when they were busy! These include Frank Hamer, Harry Fraser, Jamie Gauge and Walter Keeler. To *Ceramics Monthly* for acting as contact with and courier to American potters.

To Murray Fieldhouse who thought the whole thing was a good idea in the first place and Linda Lambert of A & C Black who saw its potential and has seen it through to the end.

Lastly, to my wife Lynne, a non-potter, who has read and re-read the manuscript without hint of boredom and has suffered the dining room looking like the aftermath of a freak storm in a paper factory as it doubled as my study.

I am sure there are some I have missed and to them my apologies along with my thanks.

Preface

Curiosity and a resilient attitude towards unpleasant shocks, are of more use in the making of glazes than a wagon load of analyses.

K.P.B.

Almost for as long as potters have made high fired 'stoneware' pots they have used wood ash to glaze them, either on its own or as one of a number of materials that were combined to form a glaze 'recipe' or formula. Almost for as long as I have been making pots I have been interested in the idea that whenever possible it is a good thing to use whatever is around me to create my work. In the beginning this assertion grew merely from an intuitive notion that these materials were there, they were free (or so I thought!) and as a principle it was an interesting way to proceed. Latterly, although all these reasons are still as valid now as they were then, I have come to realise that it is only by creating an intimate relationship with a limited but versatile number of materials that one begins to discover new depths of understanding in terms of what making pots really means.

Some of the earliest Chinese glazes were simple mixtures of ash and local clay and they have remained unsurpassed for their rich colour and surface quality. It is little wonder that these glazes provide such a wonderful source of inspiration and stimulation for 20th-century potters two and a half thousand years on. If this book is about the use of wood ash as a glaze material, it is also about taking pottery making away from the glossy catalogues and into the field and with it to experience that process of self discovery as you begin to understand the nature of your surroundings.

We all have within us the ability to make, or learn to make, a pot. Some of us develop the ability to make very good pots. Only very few have the gifts required to make *great* pots and it is true that without exception the truly great potters, whether in 15th-century Korea, 12th-century China or 20th-century England, have all had a feeling for, and understanding of, the materials around them.

As a student at college I can distinctly remember labouring under the misapprehension that the three glaze buckets containing the then almost obligatory Oatmeal, Tenmoku and Brown of indeterminate origin were all the choice there was. Upon finding a dusty, long abandoned copy of Bernard Leach's *A Potter's Book*, it came as something of a revelation to me that the world, it seemed, had been created with potters in mind. Glaze making, from then on, became an exciting adventure. Journeys down to the Towy Estuary to collect estuarine mud (on one occasion, I remember, this almost resulted in my demise as I became stuck fast in the path of an incoming tide) were followed by visits to quarries and even a coal-burning power station. All in the pursuit of materials that would lend themselves to being included in a stoneware glaze.

On November 6th 1970 my travels eventually led me to the smouldering remains of one of the previous night's bonfires and my first bucket of wood ash. My fascination with wood ash has lasted ever since.

My pottery is situated 1000 ft. above sea level overlooking the Wye Valley in deepest mid-Wales. We are surrounded by trees of many and varied species and that early fascination with the effects of wood ash in glazes has flowered into an obsession. I

A small bowl with an added pouring lip, 5" high.
This typically robust little bowl was made recently at Mashiko in Japan and is covered in a variation of the 'Nuka' glaze which is said to have first appeared in Japanese ceramics in old Karatsu wares as early as the late 16th century and in China during the Song period around AD 1000.

In this case the normally white or slightly blue chun 'Nuka' has been transformed to a ginger colour by the inclusion of a small amount of iron probably in the form of an iron-bearing stone. Hamada made extensive use of the glaze which is made from rice husk ash, a stone not unlike Cornish stone and wood ash in roughly equal proportions.

am indeed very lucky to do what I do and to live where I live and, like many other rural craftsmen, these two aspects of my life, my work and my immediate surroundings, have become inexorably linked. I rely on the countryside in a number of ways but largely to supply one of my most important materials.

I have often heard it said that potters have masochistic natures and I think it's probably true. There are not many areas of human endeavour which require such dedication and obsessive commitment. The hours are long, the work is often physically demanding and the financial rewards are less than exciting. Why is it then that a certain number choose to make things even harder for themselves by finding and preparing their own materials?

In days gone by there was no choice. Potteries grew up where the required materials occurred naturally. Potters dug their clay, crushed it, washed it, dried it, made their pots, glazed them and fired them all on the same site. In the Far East, where high temperature pottery was made some three thousand years before we managed it in the West, distinctly different types of ware evolved according to the availability of raw materials locally. Potters came to have a pride in their materials while their pots were recognised by their geographically-induced variations. They also developed a deep and intimate understanding of how these materials behaved. It was not the why but the how that was important. The knowledge that a certain material behaved in a certain way was a father's bequest to his son and then his son's son. The bond between these potters and their materials, whether it was in the Far East, medieval Europe or 18th-century Staffordshire, was similar.

Recently we seem to have lost that strong link with our materials. The changing tastes and sociological trends within our society have dictated a movement toward bright colours in ceramics, the sorts of colours not easily achieved with self-prepared materials, but those obtained quickly and easily with products that pander to the slick and the quick. Laziness and convenience in our easy come, easy go, throwaway society have also played their part.

Do not misunderstand me, it is a marvellous thing that we, as potters, can buy everything that we need to make our pots from the potters' merchants. We are free from the laborious, time-consuming chore of gathering and refining materials, *if*

we choose to be. After all, even the most independent of potters probably won't be able to discover and refine all his own materials, there simply aren't enough hours in the day. The pity of this is that many people who make pots now have little idea exactly what the powders, that arrive neatly packaged and labelled, really are and even less about where they came from and how they were found.

Those potters that I have met, some of whom you'll meet later in the book, who choose to explore the earth's mineral storeroom for themselves, display common values. As people they tend to be fiercely independent with characters as individual as their pots. They display an almost fanatical loyalty to their chosen methods but above all they have inquisitive natures, a deeply held desire to discover and succeed without having been led. It is my belief that it is only when there exists a sufficient depth of understanding of one's chosen materials that pots can be made that truly begin to glow.

Of course, not all potters live close to useful mineral deposits or granite quarries nor do they have the necessary space or equipment to cope with the material even if they did. Of all the materials of use to us, wood and vegetable ash are available to urban and country potter alike, are easily processed with little equipment and provide infinite scope for personal development.

Since those early days as a student I now know a little more about the material that has dominated my pot making for almost twenty years, and still I feel as though I've hardly begun. Such is the immense scope of the subject. In writing this book my intention is to inspire others to follow a path of personal exploration, the reasons can be their own.

Katherine Pleydell-Bouverie, a former student of Bernard Leach, devoted the best part of her potting life to investigating the merits or otherwise of the ash of the numerous trees, shrubs and plants that grew in the woods and gardens surrounding her home and pottery at Coleshill. For her, the reasons for a lifetime of research were to provide sustenance for an inquisitive nature and to utilise a material that was essentially free and that otherwise would have been left discarded.

I should like to add another reason, fun.

Any programme of experimentation should be a lot of fun. Wood and vegetable ashes vary immensely from plant to plant and from species to species. Results are seldom predictable and very often difficult to repeat but it is the unexpected that provides the excitement.

Seth Cardew has his pottery at Wenford Bridge near St. Breward in Cornwall and, like his father Michael, makes as much use as is possible of materials local to him for his clay bodies and glazes.

The glaze on this jug is as follows:

*1	Wenford frit	25
*2	Fremington clay	4
	Talc	2
	Quartz	6
*3	Meldon stone	6
	Ball clay	8
*4	Grass ash	4

*1 Wenford frit is the clinker that forms around the mousehole air inlet to the firebox of the wood-fired kiln. This clinker is a fused wood ash that still contains all its alkaline fluxes now in a glassy insoluble form, hence the term frit. Seth ball mills this residue for 8 hours to achieve a fine particle size.

*2 Fremington clay is a red earthenware from north Devon.

*3 Meldon stone is similar to a Cornish stone and comes from a quarry near Okehampton. Seth calcines the stone to 900°C and then ball mills for 8 hours.

*4 The grass ash came from a haystack that was thoroughly burnt. The ash was washed several times and then ball milled for 4 hours.

The result of all this effort is a glossy, dark glaze. This particular jug has been dipped into a white slip prior to glazing. The energetic iron oxide brushwork has become a lustrous 'kaki' red and glows in front of an olive green background.

As Katherine Pleydell-Bouverie once said, 'The point of using ashes at all, as I have found it, is that, they do sometimes produce textures that can be interesting, unusual, with luck, even beautiful. But not always. By no means always.'

For some years, during the summer months, we have run a series of courses for potters here at the pottery. Over the years people from all over the world have been our students. Many of them had never had any experience of using ashes before. Many have left us enthralled and enthused. I have seen since the results of experiments with such diverse plants as vine prunings from a potter in France, and glazes made from the ash of the prickly pear cactus from Malta. One potter from Belgium uses grass; another from Malta uses the ash from the firebox of a fellow potter's wood-fired kiln, the firing of which is supplemented with the discarded computer readouts from the Maltese Government which arrive at the pottery by the lorry load! All of these people are exploring a material that is personal to them, each contributing to the greater knowledge, each extracting immense satisfaction and all knowing that whatever they achieve is theirs alone. And lastly, all feeling that they belong to the great historical, ceramic chain of events.

A Brief History of Wood Ash Glazes

The histories of all ceramic traditions throughout the world begin with earthenwares. Often these were very low-fired as with the Neolithic funerary wares of the British Isles and Western Europe or the pots of the Jomon period from Japan. In this respect China was no exception.

Early Kilns

These soft earthenwares were fired in simple, even primitive, beehive updraught kilns or sometimes without the use of a kiln at all, merely a bonfire with the pots at its centre. This is often the case today in many parts of Africa, particularly in Nigeria where huge grain and water jars are successfully fired by this method. It was the ability of the Chinese potters, partly due to the nature of the geology of their surroundings, to develop this primitive technology and eventually to produce high-fired wares and 'stoneware' glazes.

The earliest known pottery of the Chinese culture is the unglazed earthenware of the Neolithic period. It originated sometime in the fifth millenium BC and continued to be made in one form or another until as late as the time of the birth of Christ. The pottery styles and techniques changed slowly over the centuries. However, as kilns improved so the temperatures that potters were able to attain increased. Eventually during the latter part of the Shang dynasty (c. 16th century BC) kiln technology improved to the extent that temperatures of around 1200°C became possible. It was at this time that the popular black earthenwares gave way to a greyer, denser pottery that was higher

fired for a longer period and was less reduced than the black wares.

This improvement in the understanding of kiln construction and its effect on the temperatures attained was closely linked to the rapid development of the metal-refining industry at that time. Another development of that period was the cross draught kiln. This was a direct result of the geology of the Orient; the abundance of ready-to-use stoneware clays meant that the potteries could be built on the site of the clay source. Through the centuries potters had come to realise that the more enclosed the kiln became, the hotter the firing and the more durable the finished pots. In a development from the simple deep pit kiln, the potters utilised the nearby hills and banks of clay, and hollowed out holes large enough for a man to enter. The main cavity was widened and then tapered back into a chimney leading back to the ground surface. The floor of the chamber was levelled in terraces and a fire of increasing intensity was allowed to burn at the entrance for a number of weeks which effectively biscuit-fired the inside surface of the 'cavern'. This was known as a 'bank' kiln. Pots could be stacked inside and the flame passed around them on its journey from the firebox to the chimney flue. It was this chimney that provided the extra pull or draught to the fire that increased the efficiency of the kiln and in turn raised the temperatures available to the potters.

As we now know, the bank kiln eventually gave way to the tunnel kiln built largely above ground as one long, sloping, continuous chamber. This design led to even higher temperatures but produced rather uneven heat distribution. To overcome this

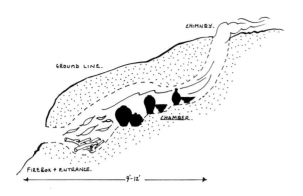

The bank kiln

problem, the long, single chamber was divided into separate compartments with inlet and outlet flues at the bottoms of the dividing walls. This system, although still essentially a cross draught configuration, introduced a downdraught in each chamber. This provided greater evenness of heat distribution and even higher temperatures due to the action of the slope-induced draught and hot gases remaining in the kiln for a longer period.

Tunnel or tube kiln

Multi-chambered climbing kiln

All this was in stark contrast to the practice of potters in Western Asia and the Middle East who continued, in many places even to the present day, to rely on a simple, beehive updraught kiln. This structure, originally just a pit into which the pots

were loaded along with some fuel was later improved by raising the floor of the chamber over the firebox. However, the system is highly inefficient and temperatures above or even approaching 1100°C were rare. In Europe, it wasn't until the 17th century that stoneware temperatures (over 1200°C) were achieved in large 'beehive' bottle kilns. I recently saw a huge updraught kiln fired in Malta and although the potter was largely ignorant of even the basic principle of kiln firing, the kiln struggled to a temperature of around 950°C having used the largest pile of wood I think I have ever seen!

So it can be seen that the development of glazes in the Far East is inextricably linked to the development of kilns and the ability of the potters to fire them efficiently. If the Far East and the Middle East were geologically reversed, that is to say that clay had been an abundant material in the eastern Mediterranean, perhaps we would have had the Persians to thank for our stonewares and the Chinese for alkaline blues.

Early Chinese Glazes

It is certain that ash glazed pottery made its first appearance sometime during the Shang period (c. 1500 BC). The introduction of glazing into the technical repertoire marks an important step forward. Pots not only became harder, more durable and of course impermeable but a coloured, glassy coating opened up new avenues of aesthetic interest. No longer were potters limited to painting with iron onto rather dry, dusty surfaces. Very soon new approaches to decoration began to evolve that took advantage of the flowing, pooling characteristics of the high-lime ash glazes.

In the first instance, however, these 'glazes' were produced accidentally, the product of white hot wood ash being carried through the kiln with the draught of the fire and falling onto the pots. As soon as the temperature reached around 1170°C the ash reacted with the surface of the clay to form a crude, often runny glaze. The build-up of these flashed areas did not rely upon the falling wood ash particles alone to form the glaze. In burning the wood fuel at such high temperatures the oxides of potassium and calcium are liberated as volatile gases which react with the silica in a clay in much the same way as the soda in a salt firing. This accounts for the well-glazed areas that occur on the vertical

Yue ware jar of the late 3rd Century AD.
The pale green glaze, probably a mixture of wood ash and
the body clay, serves to highlight the impressed patterns
and modelled relief.
Ashmolean Museum, Oxford

walls of pots. The greenish yellow colouring is due to the presence of both iron and titanium oxides in clays and ashes. Potters would have also noticed that fusible clays were melting in the higher temperatures and the appearance of kiln slag on the internal surfaces of the kiln.

To us, in retrospect, it would appear that the next step in the glazing evolutionary chain would have been but a simple one. However, it was some time before the potters realised the potential of what they had achieved. Nevertheless, it was probably before the end of the Shang period and certainly during the Zhou dynasty (1066–221 BC) that pots were produced that carried a true glaze, one that had been deliberately applied prior to the pot being placed in the kiln.

These earliest of glazes were probably mixtures of wood ash and clay and we can deduce that the mixture must have been applied in a variety of different ways perhaps depending on the site at which the pot was made. As is today, techniques probably varied in the different pottery areas. A pot of the Zhou period illustrated in Sato's book *Chinese Ceramics* (plate 17) seems to have been glazed with a 'wet' mixture either brushed on or dipped and yet the stoneware jars of the later Western Han period which have come to be known as Proto-Porcelain or Proto-Yue wares seem to have been glazed by the sifting of a dry ash and clay mixture over the still damp pots. Only the shoulders of the pot on the outside and the inside of the flared neck are glazed. A tell-tale sign is that there are often traces of glaze on the internal bases of these pots which must have fallen there during the sifting process. The bands of raised decoration are both decorative and practical in that they prevent the low silica glaze from running down and sticking the pot to the kiln.

A stoneware jar of the Western Han period 1st century BC.–1st Century AD. The upper portion of the pot is covered with a dark olive ash glaze that runs and pools in hollows and gathers on ledges. The absence of glaze on the lower portion and evidence of glaze on the internal base suggests that dry wood ash or a wood ash and clay mixture may have been dusted over the damp pot prior to firing.

The decoration is of combed wavy patterns and stylised drawings of birds and the handles are an echo from contemporary bronze work.

Ashmolean Museum, Oxford.

A Yue ware 'chicken spouted ewer' of the Southern Dynasties period (AD 420–589). Probably the most distinctive of the Yue utilitarian shapes, the chicken spouted ewer was a completely new form originated by the makers of Old Yue wares.

Ashmolean Museum, Oxford.

The large jars of the Han Dynasty (207 BC–AD 220) with their dark purplish brown body and the rich, fluid, simple ash/clay glazes have a majesty and presence all of their own. The very crudeness of the glazes imparts a special character to the pots. However, it wasn't until the development of the Yue kilns during the Eastern Han period that glaze technology took further steps forward and the potters began to better understand the contributions of the various ingredients to the glaze melt. The result was glazes that were better balanced in their oxides and were therefore less prone to running, resulting in a thicker, more uniform covering than previously. It is possible, although not certain,[1] that the introduction of a siliceous stone into the clay and ash or clay, ash and limestone mixture contributed to this new, superior finish. The stone, probably a feldspar or a stone somewhat similar to our Cornish stone, was high in silica but contained some of the fluxing oxides within itself. It is these ash-feldspar-clay[2] glazes that interest me most.

They occur again, much later, in certain Thai pottery and in the Old Seto pots from Japan where again, like their Chinese counterparts almost two thousand years before, the potters achieved a relationship of glaze, body and form that was truly special. It was a relationship that spoke of the earth, and of natural materials, impurities and all. Whilst the glazes were technically inferior to the later Song celadons and the forms sometimes a little wayward, they have a special appeal for me. I sense a personal message of potter to potter contact that transcends the centuries.

There was a rapid decline in the production of old Yue ware soon after the end of the Sui dynasty and it had more or less ceased completely by the middle of the 8th century or the middle Tang period. Glazes containing wood ash as the predominant flux continued on well into the 10th century. The glazes were similar to those of the old Yue wares except that the clay bodies in the north and their glazes were lighter in colour than the Yue ware due to the presence of less iron.

During the 8th and 9th centuries the ash glaze was placed over a iron-bearing slip and then oxidised to produce a straw-coloured finish reminiscent of lower fired lead glazes. Pots from Tongguan and a similar ware from Qionglai were decorated with brushwork in iron and copper that shows signs of soft diffused edges on the surface of the pot. This is a sure sign that the glazes contained a relatively high lime content. However, with the passing of the Yue wares it was, in China at least, the last of those ash celadon-type glazes with that special colour and fluidity that seems to say so much about the inherent qualities of wood ash as a glaze material.

Stoneware model of a dog in a pen. Ash glazed Yue ware, Jin Period.
As well as the many different utilitarian forms that were produced by the Old Yue potters there were also small models such as this. Made as toys or for inclusion with the dead in the tomb, many farmyard animals appear as charming, life-like representations.
Ashmolean Museum, Oxford.

1   Nigel Wood is of the opinion that no stone was used and that the glazes were mixtures of ash, clay and limestone. He feels that siliceous stone was not used in Southern greenware glazes until the 'kinuta' lonquan wares got started in the late 12th century.

2   Some recent work on the analyses of the glazes which have come to be known collectively as 'Greenware' (a slightly ambiguous term as far as we potters are concerned) or Yue wares, has cast some doubt as to the use of wood ash as the main flux. In some quarters it is felt that limestone was the favoured material. The Chinese certainly knew all about the properties of limestone: it was slaked for use as a mortar in the building industry and therefore readily available. However, there is some uncertainty in this area. Some pots have an opalescence, a chun-blue opacity, where the glaze has run a little thicker. This would suggest the presence of phosphorus pentoxide (P_2O_5) and therefore a wood ash. Indeed, recent analyses show a phosphorus content of at least 1% with some manganese. I tend to think that both materials were used. It seems to me that the potters would have used what was most readily available to them, the cheapest or most easily prepared, whether that was ash or limestone and to a certain extent the material that their fathers and grandfathers had used.

Stoneware vase by James Walford, 1954, 4½" high

In the early 1950s English potter James Walford became interested in reproducing some of the earliest Chinese glazes such as those on the magnificent jars of the Han dynasty. This small vase has a glaze of red clay and elm ash in the proportion of 1:3. The 'stringing' on the surface of the glaze is typical of a glaze with a high ash content and can be seen on many Chinese examples where wood ash was mixed with the body clay used by the potters to form their glazes.

By courtesy of the Board of Trustees of the Victoria & Albert Museum

Wood ash remained an important glaze flux for many centuries, certainly until the beginning of the 17th century but as time went by the glazes showed less and less evidence of an ash content. Indeed there is some disagreement amongst glaze historians as to the presence of wood ash at all in some of the later Ming glazes for instance. It is fairly certain that, as with most crafts that are handed from father to son, the habits of the country potters changed very slowly if at all. The pots that were made in their thousands for everyday use either at the table or in the kitchen or even for the packaging of consumables would have used ash as the glaze flux. After all, it was abundant and easy to prepare (unlike limestone) and free. I have seen small celadon jars of the Ming period that were originally made to store cosmetics that showed staining around the edge of the glaze line in the unglazed body. This is a sure sign that soluble alkalis existed in the glaze slop and therefore it is likely that ash had been used as all or part of the flux.

Wood ash or to be more precise the ash from rice straw is thought to have been used to produce two particular glaze effects during the 13th century. The Jun wares from the northern province of Henan relied on the highly siliceous nature of the ash to produce an opaque glaze with varying degrees of bluishness. This blue colour, the elusive chun glaze, is the product of the refraction of light as it is reflected from within the glaze rather than any pigment added to the glaze. There is some argument as to how this effect is seen. Some authorities believe that the silica rich ash is a major factor whilst others, while not disputing the contribution of silica, believe that the silica came from siliceous rocks or stones and doubt the inclusion of rice straw ash as there is little rice grown in the north of China where these particular pots were made. Nobody doubts the presence of ash (analyses show a P_2O_5 content) but its silica content remains unclear.

There is a body of informed opinion that suggests that the separation of silica-rich and lime-rich glasses on cooling create a glaze layer rather like an oil-based salad dressing after a vigorous shake. Thousands of spherical glass particles in suspension render the glaze translucent and reflective of blue light. Others argue that the glaze behaves in this fashion because of a residue of undissolved silica suspended within the glaze and the effect is encouraged by the phosphorus content of the ash

It is certainly true that I can achieve quite strong chun effects with a high silica ash glaze of roughly equal proportions of ash, feldspar and quartz but it is also true that I often accidentally achieve a chun in the bottom of bowls where the glaze has run a little thick, particularly with beech ash, in a glaze that is rather low in silica. This opalescence, I am sure, is to do with the phosphoric content of the ash and the inability of phosphoric glass to mix homogeneously with a silica glass.

The second effect worth mentioning was the technique of overlaying a layer of rice straw ash onto a tenmoku to create a mottled pattern. This was sometimes done by simply splashing it on and at other times by using a sophisticated stencil system or possibly a resist. Known as Jizhou ware I can see no real problems in duplicating this tech-

15

nique today by the use of an ash mixed with quite large quantities of quartz (possibly as much as 80% or 90%) or by the duplication of rice straw ash, the method of which I will explain later in the book (see p. 32).

Stoneware teabowl. Jizhou ware, Southern Song period, 13th Century.
The 'tortoise-shell' effect of Jizhou bowls was created by splashing a straw ash glaze over a black glaze.
    Ashmolean Museum, Oxford.

Japanese Ash Glazes

It took almost 2000 years before the kiln technology that had allowed the Chinese potters to reach the temperatures necessary to melt the fly ash in the kilns eventually reached the Japanese. Their Sueki wares which, like the Han dynasty jars, show signs of having had the ash dusted over them prior to firing were the first step toward the more sophisticated wares of Old Seto. However, unlike the Chinese who saw the cruder ash flashing and early ash/clay glazes as a mere stepping stone on the path of development, the Japanese developed an aesthetic around these pots which gave rise to the other ancient kilns at Tamba, Bizen and Shigaraki. These unglazed pots which rely on the kindness of the kiln and an intuitive knowledge of the 'right' place in the kiln for their impromptu decoration continue to be made today.

The Old Seto glazes were, again, simple clay and ash mixtures. In Japan, we can be quite sure of this because of the known absence of limestone. Also, the green or sometimes straw yellow glazes show the typical qualities which one would associate with high calcia glazes. The best examples of these glazes have a light, fresh green that runs softly into the

A jar and stand, Sueki ware, 5th Century Japan.
For Japan, Sueki was a ware of an entirely new type, unlike any ceramics that had appeared previously but bearing a marked resemblance to some of the pots of the Shang and Western Zhou periods from China almost two thousand years previously. To begin with, the glazing was the accidental effect of the firing but later examples show signs of the ash glazes having been dusted over the damp pots prior to placing in the kiln.
    Ashmolean Museum, Oxford.

decorations of stamped and drawn patterns. The bold and sure drawing of foliage and applied ridges and sprigging all serve to highlight the fluid glaze and bring the surface to life. Other glazes were of darker hue, mixtures of ash with iron-bearing stones, and some are straw coloured having been oxidised in the fire. These pots have been a source of inspiration to me since I first saw pictures of them in a book almost twenty years ago and for me surpass the Song and Yuan dynasty Qingbai bottles from where the original inspiration came.

Wood ash as a flux for high-fired stoneware glazes has been central to the development of Eastern pottery. It is remarkable, given the relatively close proximity to China and the established trading links that existed, that almost two thousand years elapsed before the first high-fired ash glazes appeared in Japan, Korea and Thailand. Similarly, although wood ash has remained an important feature of glazes in the Far East ever since and indeed, was the major ingredient of the lower-fired ash-rich alkaline frits that formed the basis of Islamic glazes, as far as the West is concerned it wasn't until the beginning of the 20th century and the development of a craft movement that looked Eastward for its inspiration that it became a material worthy of investigation. That is, with one interesting exception.

Ash Glazes of the South East United States

In the late 18th and the 19th centuries, salt was the predominant glaze used on North American stoneware in all areas except the South East. Here in the very early 19th century a distinctly different regional type of alkaline glaze evolved. In the Carolinas, where a strong pottery tradition had already established itself by the end of the 18th century, the potters began to use a glaze based on the wood ash from the firemouths of the kilns. This wood ash was mixed, as in the early Chinese glazes, with a local red clay and sometimes with small quantities of quartz, feldspar and powdered glass.

The glazes have all the qualities one might expect from a high ash content and they bear a strong resemblance to the Han dynasty glazes and those of the Sueki period and the Old Seto in Japan. Nobody is quite sure how this technology reached the American South East and theories abound as to how information about the Chinese ways could have reached the colony. There is some evidence to suggest that wood ash had been used as a glaze flux in some French pottery from the 18th century and that a migrant potter may have taken with him this knowledge. I feel that the inquisitive potter is often underestimated by the non-potting academic observer and that it is quite possible that the American potters made the same discoveries for themselves that the Chinese potters had two and a half thousand years before. It would have only required the overfiring of a kiln of the then common lead-glazed ware to have melted some of the fly ash and a clever potter to realise that this occurrence might have the potential to supersede the harmful lead glazes. In any event, the pots that were produced are amongst some of the most beautiful utilitarian pots in the 'modern' world and though the shapes that carry the flowing, richly coloured glazes are essentially European in character, some of them bear an uncanny resemblance to the bulbous jars made in China, Korea and later in Japan.

Jar, Alkaline glazed stoneware, 16" high.
This jar from South Carolina has a glaze of a sand and wood ash mixture and is thought to have been potted and decorated by black slave labour. The trailing is in kaolin. The 'stringing' of the glaze surface is typical of a high ash glaze.
Courtesy, Museum of Early Southern Decorative Arts, Winston-Salem, N.C.

The 20th-Century Contribution

A tall vase by Bernard Leach.
The glaze is composed of equal parts of clay (a red earthenware) and hardwood ash and is an Indian red colour breaking to ochre where it has run a little thicker. The characteristic changes of colour serve to highlight the freely executed incised pattern.
Courtesy of Bonham & Sons Ltd.

I have a feeling that, in the first instance, it was a concern for authenticity in his glazes rather than any desire for the qualities of ash for its own sake that prompted Bernard Leach to begin to use wood ash at St Ives in the 1920s. Having learnt the basics of his pottery in Japan and then having brought the young Hamada back with him to England, it was inevitable, bearing in mind his fascination for all things Eastern, that he should wish to recreate as faithfully as possible the glazes that he had seen while in Japan. Later he often used high ash content glazes, particularly on tall jugs and vases. From reading the description of his own work with ashes, it is clear that he had a thorough understanding of the material. However, it was left to Katherine Pleydell-Bouverie, a former pupil of Leach's, to carry out the most thorough investigation into the behaviour of different wood ashes in modern times. From 1928 until the time of her death in 1985 she systematically tested many different plant, shrub and tree ashes and her work has formed the basis and inspiration for much further work by potters all over the world.

A large jar by Katherine Pleydell-Bouverie.
The thick, oily glaze has been brushed with an iron pigment to produce a variety of colour and texture. The glaze is made from the ash of the box shrub and is:

Box ash	35
Potash feldspar	55
Quartz	10
China clay	10

It is described by K.P.B. as a 'rather smokey grey'.

18

Wood ash remains probably the single most versatile material available to potters. At a time in history when all pottery requirements can be purchased off a shelf — a situation non-existent in the past, and I suspect, in the future — wood ash provides potters with the opportunity to explore material that, in the truest sense, belongs to the earth and to the individual. Perhaps, more importantly, it provides us with a direct link to the potters of the past and a means, not just of being able to recreate quiet, subtle and beautiful glazes or even that we are in charge of our own scheme of work, but of feeling that we are truly part of the ceramic order of things.

Katherine Pleydell-Bouverie photographed shortly before her death in 1985.
'I want my pots to make people think, not of the Chinese, but of things like pebbles and shells and birds' eggs and the stones over which moss grows.'
   From a letter to Bernard Leach 1930.

Small faceted bowl by the Author, 4½″ high.
With this small faceted teabowl I have alternated a pattern of engraved lines from one facet to the next to produce a chevron or herringbone effect. The bowl was then dipped in a white slip and covered in my standard ash glaze using beech.

The Growing Plant

Before we go on to deal with wood ash as a material for potters, it is as well to have at least a basic understanding of the reasons why a living, growing life form can provide us with the elements essential for glaze making. Whenever I explain to visitors at my pottery that the glazes are made, in part, from the ashes of burnt wood and straw the reaction ranges from mild surprise to disbelief.

A magnificent beech tree in the field just above the pottery.

Plant life surrounds us. The existence of vegetation is vital to the preponderance of animal life and the two life forms are inexorably linked. Both plants and animals form part of the infinite chain of growth, death and rebirth that sustains the planet.

All animal life, in common with plant life, requires certain elements to be contained within its diet. If these elements are missing or deficient then the health of the life form suffers, sometimes to the point of death. It stands to reason then, that as the animal kingdom is at the top end of the food chain, if we follow the chain down far enough we find that all the nutritional elements begin their great journey having been extracted from the earth by plants. Only to be deposited there again either by the dead and decaying plants themselves or the decaying remains of animal life.

Not being a botanist it came as a mild surprise to me, when researching this section, that one of the principal methods of plant analysis is the reduction of the plant to ash. During the process of combustion, hydrogen, oxygen, carbon and nitrogen are driven off and we are left with a non-volatile residue, the ash. In this ash we have a record of the mineral elements taken on board by the plant during its life and an indication as to the type of soil in which the plant grew.

It follows then, that the elements which, on analysis, are found in plant ash must be the constituents of their food. Those inorganic elements (the ones we are concerned with) that have been traced are potassium, sodium, magnesium, calcium, phosphorus, sulphur, silicon, iron, chlorine, iodine, manganese, aluminium and bromine. Other elements do occur, such as copper and silver, but in such small amounts they are listed in analysis as trace or often not included at all.

Later in this book you will find some of the above elements discussed in relation to their uses and actions for the potter. Of their number, not all will concern us, their amounts contained in ashes too small to be of any consequence. Others, such as calcium and potassium are of immense importance and their relatively large percentage in the ashes of most plants is what makes plant ash such a useful and infinitely variable material for the creative potter.

As we know, plants grow, with very few exceptions, in soil. The soil serves three functions: it provides an anchorage whereby the plant is held firmly in position; it furnishes a supply of water; and it contributes the mineral salts essential to the plant's successful existence.

The bulk and the basic material of a soil is composed of small, angular particles which have been formed by the disintegration of rock. It is these particles that contribute the mineral nutrients to the plant when the water present in the soil dissolves their surfaces. The dissolved minerals are taken in by the plant via the root. The root, however cannot absorb anything that is not in solution* and while certain elements enter into solution very easily, others do not. To overcome any difficulty that the plant may have in obtaining the required nutrients, plants have developed a mechanism whereby they can dissolve rock particles by themselves. This is achieved by the secretion of an acid from the root hairs that attacks the rock particle surface. Even silica, normally thought of as insoluble, can be absorbed by this means.

I do not want to become over involved with the extremely complicated theories of how the water containing the dissolved minerals is taken in by the plant. This is not the book to deal with this subject in great detail and I would refer the reader who wishes to know more to a good botanical textbook. However, suffice it to say, that the root hairs absorb solutions from the soils by osmosis and these solutions are passed from cell to cell, via the cell wall, by osmotic action governed by the principles of diffusion. Eventually the solutes find their way to the central core of the root from where they are taken by a process of capillary action to all parts of

the plant. The capillary action is sustained by the evaporation of water from the leaf surface which, for a large tree, can be many tons during a summer. Once aboard the plant the minerals are used to help the plant perform certain functions and for the process of building tissue.

The use which a plant makes of the elements which come to it from the soil has been studied a great deal over the years. Many of the reactions that take place in a plant cell are extremely complicated and the involvement of the different chemical elements is not at all properly understood. It may be, for instance, that one element could perform more than one function within the plant depending on, for instance, the age of the plant. It is also possible that functions may differ from species to species. It is enough for us, as potters, to know that plant life gathers together a cocktail of elements in a convenient (if less than efficient in terms of usable bulk) source that, in analysis, often resembles a natural glaze.

Plant and tree ashes can vary from species to species even when growing in the same soil, while ashes of the plants of the same species can also vary if they are grown in different soils or in different climatic conditions. Plants have an ability to regulate their intake of certain minerals even when, as in the case of plants growing on salt marshes, there is an over abundance of a particular mineral.

Trees also deposit higher concentrations of certain minerals in particular areas within themselves. Calcium accumulates in large amounts in the needles of conifer trees, in the heart wood and in the bark of many trees and likewise in all organs of plants growing on soils containing much lime. The quantities of calcium in the dead bark of the oak may reach as high as 95% of the total ash. Silica is deposited in the walls of many plants and is one of the minerals where doubt still exists as to its exact purpose. It occurs as a large percentage in the ashes of many grasses and was once thought to act as a strengthener to the stem although this now seems not to be the case.

Potassium seems to gather in the young parts of the plant, the buds and young leaves, and the living tissue of the bark can often contain as much as 50% potassium. Magnesium tends to accumulate in the seeds whilst iron, again, occurs chiefly in the younger parts.

So we can see that the variability of environment for the growth of plants coupled with a less than scientific approach to the gathering of different

---

* Some authorities now believe that the plant **is** able to absorb microscopic insoluble particles through the root system providing the particle size is small enough.

wood samples by potters renders the study of ash analyses of limited use. If one sample contained rather a large proportion of bark it may be altogether different in character to another sample that was largely branch wood even though they came from the same species of tree. At best, we can make an educated assumption as to the character of an ash and its use to the potter, but more of this later. What is of real interest to us as potters is that the various types of ash contain varying amounts of the correct oxides that we require to create pottery glazes of special character and quality.

A large and rugged platter made from heavily grogged clay by Ginny and Tom Marsh USA. The central portion has been glazed with:

Mixed hardwood ash   50
Local earthenware clay   50

and relies on the ash glaze to pick out the texture created by work with a throwing rib or turning tool that has puckered the surface of the clay because of the high grog content.

What is Wood Ash?

A teabowl by Shoji Hamada.

This is the off-white glaze known in Japan as 'Nuka' and is made from the ash of the burnt husks of the rice plant. In Japan the glaze is prepared from a mixture of rice husk ash, a siliceous stone and wood ash. Rice husk ash is almost pure silica, often 95% pure and so with that in mind the glaze has been reformulated for us in the West as:

Ash	50
Feldspar	60
Quartz	40

Use this as a starting point and alter the ingredients as necessary. It is a glaze high in silica and relies, for its milky whiteness, on a surfeit of silica remaining unfluxed and suspended in the glaze melt. It requires a high firing temperature of at least 1280°C and preferably 1300°C. An analysis for rice husk ash appears at the back of this book.

Courtesy of Bonham's Ltd.

Before moving on to the business of trying to create satisfactory glazes, it is as well to pause and consider, first of all the nature of the material that we have at hand, and secondly the materials that we shall combine with it to form our glazes.

Hamada was once heard to respond to a student who commented that ash glazes was a simplistic approach by saying, with the inscrutability of the oriental, that it was, in fact, the contrary that is true. Ash glazes are the most complex of all. This was, he said, because in ashes we are dealing with nature's mixture. Hamada knew that it was pointless to try and analyse his materials too closely, it was enough to know that with careful attention to ensuring a consistent supply and great care in its preparation, nature would take care of the content. In replying to the student Hamada had known exactly what he had meant by his assertion but chose to teach him a short lesson. It is the extreme complexity of the chemical structure of an ash that insists that the material must be treated in a simplistic manner.

In the East potters were, and still are, happy to work with the materials that were at hand, accepting their impurities as an inevitable fact of life but at the same time working in harmony with them. Much of the charm of the old Eastern glazes is due to the presence of impurities that the potters couldn't or didn't want to remove. The most common of these impurities was a small percentage of iron which imparted subtle shades of pale blue or green to porcelain glazes. Today, in the West, our materials have, for the sake of industry, been refined to the point of blandness. It is also true that, in the

West, we had no tradition of country-made stone-wares as we had with the earthenwares. Such a tradition would, I am sure, have altered our whole perception as to what constituted a 'good' pot and led to the acceptance of and even glorification of the impure and the accidental. As it was, the larger pieces of Staffordshire or North Wales slipware were revered and appreciated despite their comparative crudeness of manufacture. They were 'taken care of' and often handed down through the family, spoken fondly of and eventually given honourable

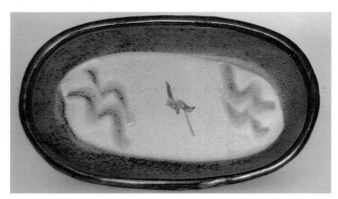

A small press moulded dish from Japan, 5" wide.

A white slip has been combed through at either end of this dish and the inside then covered in an ash glaze of equal proportions of ash and a siliceous stone a little like our Cornish stone. The outside has a tenmoku and the central motif is in green and red onglaze enamel. This dish is one of a set of six and is for serving rice at the table.

retirement. Unfortunately, our affection for the slipwares, the English Delft and latterly, the salted stonewares wasn't strong enough to prevent the ceramic industry from monopolising general tastes. Our ceramic heritage became lost in a morass of sanitised white china, porcelain and pretty flowers. By the turn of the 20th century we had, with the exception of only a handful of potteries, thrown away eight hundred years of tradition.

As I have said in the introduction to this book, wood ash provides us with the ideal material with which to make some gesture towards a return to a more natural approach in ceramics and in doing so may teach something of the humility of the Eastern potters and their regard and reverence for natural and impure materials.

Hamer states in his *Potter's Dictionary* that 'wood ash is the inorganic residue left after the combustion of the organic structure of wood, the term is popularly extended to include other vegetable ashes, e.g. grass, straw, bushes and smaller plants such as nettles'.

In wood ash we are dealing with a highly complex mineral and chemical cocktail: a mixture of solubles and insolubles, alkalis and acids of such variability as to render the formulation of an average analysis a waste of time if not an impossibility. For this reason, I believe, there is little point in worrying about the exact content of an ash; what should concern us is what that particular ash will do for us. Having said that, there is no harm in knowing what the analysis for a given ash may be. This will give you at least an idea of what you may expect from your ash sample and may make things a little easier when trying to construct a glaze.

Analyses

I have already suggested that analyses of different ash types are of limited value. The reason for this can be summed up in one word, variability. It is not the purpose of this book to become too deeply entrenched in the chemical or scientific approach to ashes. However it is important to understand that any analysis is only as good as the analyst who performs it. As Robert Tichane, an analyst himself, says 'each person has a different cutoff point with regard to the amount of effort that he is willing to put into an analysis'. From the horse's mouth so as to speak! So we have our first variable, the human element.

Next we have to look at the differing conditions in which the plant or tree grew. As I have already mentioned in the chapter concerned with the botanical aspect, plants are able to absorb mineral nutrients from the soil partly through their ability to dissolve rock particles. Although plants have an ability to regulate their intake of individual minerals it is nevertheless true that differences in ash content can occur within the same species depending on the type of soil in which they grew. Here we have our second variable.

Lastly we have to consider the quality of the sample analysed. Was it old wood or new? Was there a high proportion of bark? Was there a lot of branch wood or was it mostly trunk? Was the sample clean or was soil attached to the bark? Was it burned on a clean surface? If not, did a contamination take place from the underlying soil? The sample quality is our third variable.

If one studies the table on p. 25 it is plain that for whatever the reason differences have occurred in the results of the analyses of applewood taken from the four different sources. The best that we can say is that all four samples are very similar. If an analysis is at hand for the type of wood ash that you have, then by all means check to see the sort of effect that you may expect from it. However, you must regard this as very much a rough guideline.

Analyses of apple wood ash from four different sources.

	Cardew[1]	Pleydell-Bouverie	Leach[2]	Wolff[3]
SiO_2	2.7	1.31	4.0	1.8
Al_2O_3	–	–	3.03	–
Fe_2O_3	–	1.66	1.07	–
P_2O_5	4.5	4.9	2.43	4.5
CaO	70.9	63.6	83.00	70.9
MgO	5.5	7.46	4.98	5.45
MnO	–	–	–	–
K_2O	11.8	19.24	1.26	11.8
Na_2O	1.9	10.45	–	1.8
SO_3	2.7	0.93	–	2.7

1 *Pioneer Pottery* by Michael Cardew.
2 *A Potter's Book* by Bernard Leach.
3 *Aschen-Analysen* by Dr Emil Wolff.

It is interesting to note that although Cardew doesn't refer to Wolff's analysis it is fairly obvious that this was its original source and the analysis has been hijacked at some point! For its time Emil Wolff's investigation was a staggering achievement and it seems that it has been a reliable source of reference for over a century.

The Composition of Ashes

All types of ashes may be loosely grouped into those which are high in calcia, these tend to be the tree woods and bushes, and those which have a high silica content, largely derived from grasses and cereal crops. However, as with everything concerning ashes there are exceptions to the rules. Elder wood does tend to contain rather a high proportion of silica and, just to redress the balance, not that you'll probably ever find any, soya straw has a high

calcia and low silica content. However, as far as the potter is concerned these two groupings will help to form an understanding of how any particular ash may be expected to perform.

There has been a certain amount of information published concerning the composition of ashes which, true to the nature of the subject and the analytical difficulties we have already spoken about, has been misleading. For instance, Daniel Rhodes in *Clay and Glazes for the Potter*, asserts that wood and vegetable ashes contain 10% to 15% of alumina. I have noted that the greatest amount I have seen quoted is 0.63% in the case of ash wood. More often than not it is omitted from the analysis or is included as a trace element. He also says that 30% to 70% of silica should be expected when often there is much less, and up to 30% of lime when often there is much more. Katherine Pleydell-Bouverie claimed that ash contained from 50% to 60% of lime and silica, again this is more often not the case.

If we look at the two tables on p. 26, a truer picture emerges and the assertion made earlier that ashes can be grouped into basic and acidic or high lime or high silica is proved. Of the woods shown, the highest silica content is 15.00%. (This is a high figure when compared to other analyses that I have. I assume that this sample may have contained a high bark content which often shows a higher silica

The bowls in this photograph are each glazed with an ash glaze of exactly the same formula, the only difference is that the ash in each one is from a different tree.

On the left the ash is pine, in the middle beech and on the right walnut. In surface quality they are all fairly similar except that the pine ash glaze is more fluid. A deeper roll of glaze can be seen around the ledge on the outside of the bowl.

The greatest difference in these three examples is the colour. The pine is very much darker than the other two and the beech a little darker than the walnut.

All three are beautiful glazes but illustrate the differences that may occur from one ash to another.

level.) The lowest calcia level is willow at 20% which can be regarded as something of an exception. Most of the woods have calcia contents of around 40% and upwards with apple wood the highest shown at 63.60%. It is interesting to note that when a tree does have a low calcia content that almost invariably there is a high potash content.

The next step, with the aid of the tables, is to try and evaluate the two distinct groups and assess their contribution to the glaze. Bernard Leach in *The Potter's Book* classified ashes into three areas, which he called, Hard, Medium and Soft. He did this by examining an analysis and subtracting all those materials on the one hand which are fluxes (lime, potash, soda, magnesia etc.) from the non-fluxing fraction i.e. silica, alumina and phosphorus. Leach said that the remaining balance roughly suggested the effect of the ash in the glaze. Medium ashes are those which lie between 40 hard and minus 20 soft. If we look a little closer at this and with the help of the tables on this page we can see that, for instance, beech ash has a total of at least 83.45 on the flux side and only 9.23 on the other. This gives a total of − 74.22. Obviously this is an ash well into the 'soft' bracket and can be looked upon as having a considerable fluxing effect in the glaze. Alternatively, if

we look at the analysis for rice straw ash we find that the total for the fluxes is much lower at 9.08 whereas the silica, alumina, phosphorus content totals 87.69; this provides a final indicator of + 78.61 − a hard ash, one that, in theory anyway, will contribute much less in fluxing power to the glaze.

It is evident then that the ashes which contain the greatest proportion of calcia are those that can be regarded as strong fluxes. In practice this accounts for most of the trees and shrubs. The ashes high in silica are produced by quicker growing plants such as grasses, cereal crops, certain vegetables and nettles. Grain husks are particularly high in silica, the plant using the strength of the silica crystal as protection for the seed. Rice husk ash is one of these materials and forms the basis for Hamada's Nuka glaze, that thick, white to cream glaze so typical of his work. Cardew suggested in *Pioneer Pottery*, that some of the high silica ashes could be used as a substitute for flint or quartz in a glaze and that some of the high calcia ashes could provide an alternative to whiting or limestone.

	Apple	Beech	Oak	Pine	Spruce	Willow
Silica SiO_2	1.31	3.01	15.30	10.00	2.73	4.44
Alumina Al_2O_3	—	—	0.13	0.43	—	0.05
Phosphorus P_2O_5	4.9	6.2	13.8	8.8	2.12	10.00
Iron Fe_2O_3	1.66	0.62	2.40	4.00	1.42	1.25
Calcium CaO	63.60	42.00	30.02	25.00	33.97	20.21
Potash K_2O	19.24	24.29	14.00	26.50	19.66	49.80
Magnesia MgO	7.46	8.20	12.01	6.32	11.27	8.26
Soda Na_2O	10.45	8.34	9.12	8.65	1.37	2.50
Manganese MnO	—	4.52	0.10	5.06	22.96	0.18
Sulphates SO_3	0.93	2.10	2.61	4.63	2.64	1.22
Copper Ox CuO	—	—	0.05	—	—	—
Chlorine Cl	0.45	0.72	1.18	0.52	0.07	0.08

	Wheat straw	Rye straw	Rice straw	Lawn grass
Silica SiO_2	67.5	49.27	77.68	39.64
Alumina Al_2O_3	—	—	9.11	16.60
Phosphorus P_2O_5	4.8	6.53	0.90	9.00
Iron Fe_2O_3	0.6	1.91	2.93	3.44
Calcium CaO	5.8	8.20	4.00	12.88
Potash K_2O	13.6	22.56	1.68	6.19
Magnesia MgO	2.5	3.10	2.44	5.65
Soda Na_2O	1.4	1.74	0.96	6.20
Manganese MnO	—	—	—	—
Sulphates SO_3	—	4.25	—	—
Copper CuO	—	—	—	—
Chlorine Cl	—	2.18	—	—

A slabbed bottle by William Marshall, 7½" high.
William Marshall worked for many years at the Leach Pottery in St Ives before setting up his own workshop. This bottle was made at St Ives and is a dark olive green with a background of rich brown. It is a simple ash and clay glaze probably in equal proportions, possibly over an iron-bearing slip.
   Courtesy of Christies Ltd.

The Individual Components

Here we shall look at the various elements in the ash and the role they play. As we have seen the elements within ashes vary greatly from ash to ash but having tentatively grouped the ashes into those high in calcia and those high in silica it seems sensible to begin by considering the actions of these two materials.

Calcia, Calcium Oxide or Lime, CaO

Calcium oxide alone is a highly refractory material with a melting point of 2572°C and it is only when in combination with other oxides at temperatures over 1100°C that it becomes a flux and a strong one at that. Most of the wood ashes have a calcium content that lies somewhere between 30% and 60%, sometimes even higher, and as whiting or calcium carbonate has a calcium content of 56% we can, as Cardew suggests, regard wood ash as an impure form of and substitute for whiting. We have to remember that in a wood ash calcia appears already intimately combined with other oxides and won't, therefore, behave in quite the same way as calcia added, let's say, in the form of whiting. An excess of the purer form can produce a mattness in the glaze due to the presence of more than the required amount of oxide that can enter into the melt. Calcium has little effect on the colouring oxides although it does have a mild bleaching effect on iron oxide. It is also thought to be the cause of what I consider one of the attractions of ash celadons, namely the bleaching of the body layer immediately under the glaze. This phenomenon provides those marvellous areas of pale, almost white colour behind the top layer of bluish green.

In short we can regard any ash that is high in calcia as a major fluxing influence.

An open pot 6½" high by Warren MacKenzie.
Warren MacKenzie accompanied by his late wife Alix went to work with Bernard Leach at St Ives in 1950 and stayed for two and a half years. He now has his workshop at Stillwater, Minnesota where, as he says, 'I try to make pots as rich as possible but as quiet as possible, that is essentially what I want'.

This jar shows the influence of the Japanese tea ceremony wares and is glazed with a mixture of:

4 parts   Ash
5 parts   Albany slip or a fusible red clay
Fired to 1280°C, reduction atmosphere.

Silica, Silicon Oxide, SiO

In wood ash, silica levels are usually low and rarely amount to more than around 10%. We have to be careful here though because wood samples are not always just the pure wood. Bark nearly always has a higher concentration of silica as does the trunk wood. Branch wood may have as little as 1% content. In grasses however the story is very different. Silica levels here may reach as high as 70% and in the husks of certain grasses even higher, as much as 90%.

As we have already said, silica is the main glass-forming material and we'll be looking more closely at it as a material in its natural state a little later on. The silicon oxide derived from plant ash differs from quartz or flint in that botanic silica has an extremely fine particle size, some below a 600 mesh size and because of this seems to have the ability to flux itself. The silica that appears in wood ash is very evenly distributed and intimately combined with all the other oxides and although it makes an interesting substitute for the purer forms of silica it cannot really be regarded as a direct one.

A faceted box 5" diameter by the Author
The two parts of this pot are thrown separately and then faceted at the same time with the lid in place prior to turning. The box was then dipped in a white slip and subsequently glazed with my standard formula this time with ash wood ash. The glaze has stayed fairly matt only turning glassy where it was applied thickly in the centre of the lid. The glaze has burnt away at the edges to reveal a reddish brown which highlights the cut lines.

The alkalis

For the purposes of this study I have grouped the three remaining alkalis together. Having already dealt with the calcia fraction we are now left with the potash (K_2O), magnesia (MgO), and soda (Na_2O). All are alkaline and have a fluxing action upon silica. Potassium oxide, or as it is more commonly called potash, behaves in a similar way to soda, the two of them, with lithia, are the three strong alkaline fluxes in glaze making. They are both highly soluble, soda being the slightly more soluble of the two, and can be detected in the glaze slop by a soft, soapy feeling to the water. As we have already mentioned, their high alkaline state renders them caustic. For this reason it is best not to put the hands into an ash slurry or ash glaze slop. Both potash and soda melt at relatively low temperatures, at 700°C and 900°C, and will flux silica alone at temperatures below 800°C.

Magnesium oxide rarely appears in amounts over 15% in wood or vegetable ashes although certain conifers including pine and larch are an exception. Its action is similar to that of calcia in that it is a flux from around 1170°C onwards. Because, in the case of magnesia, we are not talking about very high percentages it behaves as a flux only and its potential as an opacifier and its ability to render a glaze smooth and buttery in texture are never seen.

Phosphorus pentoxide, P_2O_5

This is a glass-forming oxide that is present in all plant ashes. Indeed, phosphorus, in the form of phosphates, is essential to the healthy growth of any plant. The presence of phosphorus in the analysis of certain Chinese glazes is regarded as an indication that ashes were used in the glaze make up. Phosphorus rarely represents more than a few tenths of 1% of raw earth materials but because of the plant's ability to absorb and accumulate the minerals it requires over prolonged periods phosphorus may represent as much as 3% of the ash.

Phosphorus can be responsible for a chun effect in glazes. This occurs because the phosphoric glass cannot mix homogeneously with the silica glass and is left therefore suspended in droplets throughout the glaze layer where it refracts the light because of its minute particle size. The effect, even in the hands of an expert, is unpredictable and takes very careful attention to the firing schedule for any success at all.

I have often noticed a bluish flush in the bottom of bowls or wide dishes where the glaze may have run and gathered as a thickness and I have found that it tends to happen with beech ash more than any other. This is surprising in that beech ash has less phosphorus pentoxide than, for instance, pine ash. I have also noticed that the bluish flush happens more often when the beech ash glaze is over a white slip containing China clay. For me, the effect is pleasing only when it happens now and again; it is one of those spectacular gifts of the kiln which, were it to happen more often, could easily outstay its welcome.

The colouring oxides

Of the colouring oxides present in plant ashes only iron and manganese are really worthy of consideration. Titania, vanadium, copper and chromium can all be present in trace amounts at different times but the amounts are so small they are often not shown in analysis and play no part in the colour of the glaze. Iron may be present, depending on the ash, in amounts up to 15% in certain plants but more usually, in wood ash, the figure is between 0.5% and 2.5%. In the case of manganese, the percentages present are sometimes startling. One analysis that I have quotes 22.96% for spruce ash and yet as little as 0.1% for oak. Tichane suggests that because of the form that the manganese takes it is ineffective as a colourant. He says that it is more effective in oxidation and may account for the amber tint of many oxidised ash glazes rather than the iron content.

Alumina, Al_2O_3

Whilst alumina is one of the most important oxides in ceramics, it hardly figures at all in plant ashes. Occasionally, there may be a content of up to 5% but more often than not it isn't quoted in the analysis.

Other elements

Of the other elements present in ashes there is little to be said in this context because either their amount or their action is so limited as to render them irrelevant. Elements, as they are found in ashes, differ from the same elements found in minerals only in their particle size and their resulting intimate combination with each other. As we shall see in a later chapter it is perfectly possible to re-create 'ash glazes' by the use of minerals alone, although I have to say, I see little virtue in this practice. Ash is a material in its own right and not a 'low-tech' substitute for refined commercially available minerals. Ash glazes have qualities that a synthetic substitute can never match although I'm quite prepared to accept that there is a place for them and I shall discuss it further later on in the book.

Collecting and Preparing Wood Ash

Wood Ash Doesn't Grow on Trees – Locating your Ash

In using any type of 'local' material the first concern is to locate a supply that will, hopefully, last a reasonable length of time. This will enable you to test the material thoroughly, achieve some success and still have enough left over to use in your glazes for a prolonged period. With local stones and clays this usually isn't a problem. Once located, there is more often than not an inexhaustible supply. This is not really the case with wood ash. Even when a supply can be located that promises to go on for some time there is little guarantee that the ash will remain constant in its make up and it will probably require constant adjustment.

If I tell you that for every 100 lbs of dry wood that are burnt you will be lucky to gather 8 ozs of usable ash, you may begin to appreciate the quantity of wood that must be burnt to enable the potter to use high ash content glazes in any sort of commercial way.

In my house I have two stoves that burn nothing but wood as fuel. I have another in my workshop. During an average winter I burn approximately 9 tons of wood and this provides me with enough ash to use all the year round with only a small surplus. So you can see that to try and create your own ash purely to use in glazes and not as a by-product of heating your home could be an awesome task apart from being environmentally doubtful. It is far better to locate a supply where the ash is a by-product of some industrial or agricultural process and is regarded as waste.

Even though I am essentially 'self-sufficient' in wood ash if I choose to be, I cannot burn the variety of woods that really make life interesting and I have to look elsewhere for ash that I cannot produce for myself. I tend to burn pine in the greatest quantity because that is what I can obtain in large amounts. Pine ash is perfectly O.K. but I have no desire to work with one ash alone. The hardwoods such as oak, beech and ash have less iron content and therefore produce a green glaze much lighter in tone and with a fresher, cleaner colour than the pine. It is a fact that even situated where I am these hardwoods are not easy to come by and I rely on a number of different people collecting their ashes for me.

For those potters whose output isn't on a commercial level or for those who use only small quantities of ash, there may be the opportunity to burn wood that has no other destiny than to be discarded. This may be some prunings from a bush or a hedge, it could be reclaimed timber from a building project or some grass clippings which may not provide enough ash for a prolonged period but will, even if the quantity is small, provide the opportunity for some experiments from which the experience and the knowledge gained can be carefully noted and then stored for future reference.

Recently, I was given a small sample of walnut ash from a tree that had been uprooted in a storm. I duly tested it and found that it produced a particularly fine glaze, a pale blue/green of exceptional freshness. Unfortunately, there was only enough left to cover a handful of pots and I was quite convinced that I would be unable to obtain any further supply. However, the results of the tests were recorded for future reference. Only two months later a large walnut tree was felled no more than 200 yards from my pottery and I was able to purchase it for firewood. This was one of those chance happenings that come along all too infrequently but one that does serve to illustrate the usefulness, let alone the fun, of testing even the smallest samples of different types of ashes.

In a moment I shall describe the best method of burning wood so as to retain the ash and its quality, plus, how to burn and extract the greatest possible amount of usable ash from any given amount of wood. First though, some suggestions as to where you might find large supplies of ash and be thanked for taking it away.

Ash Sources

As I have already mentioned I am to all intents and purposes self-sufficient in wood ash — only variety is lacking. Working on the principle that I rarely say no to anything that is offered to me free of charge, there are a number of kind, usually pot-loving people who are only to pleased to collect their ash for me. Households with wood burning stoves have always been my most productive source. They tend to burn only hardwoods which is important for me because I tend to burn mostly pine.

Wood stoves are becoming increasingly popular, not only in rural areas, but also in large towns. One only has to supply a metal container and a regular, usually fairly constant, supply of ash is yours. Often you will find that these ashes contain nails and other extraneous pieces of metal which, apart from adding a little iron oxide to the mixture, are easily sieved out and are really nothing to worry about.

Sometimes a single wood is used as people have to accept what the log suppliers are cutting at any particular time although I find that when a mixture is burnt it tends to continue to be the same mixture over a prolonged period.

There are two things to be careful of when obtaining your ash this way. First, ensure that there has been *no* burning of coal or anthracite in with the wood. Coal has a very high silica content and more than the usually required amount of iron (sometimes as much as 11%) and although coal ash can be used as a glaze material (see pp. 61–65), it needs to be considered as a single material rather than as an addition or contaminant to wood ash.

Secondly, try to make sure that your ash source is free from calcined bones. It is quite common for

A massive storejar by Jim Malone.

This huge pot is over two feet in height and having made some fairly large pots myself I know the difficulties involved in making work on this sort of scale. The glaze is made from hawthorn ash collected after a farmer had completed a new hedge. Jim Malone lives in Cumbria and makes extensive use of local materials. The recipe for the glaze on this jar is:

Shap hornfels	25
Shap pink granite	75
Hawthorn ash	100
Ball clay	50

which is a 'localised version of the Leach standard:

Ash	40
Feldspar	40
Clay	20

Try substituting feldspar for the granite and hornfels and adding a small percentage of iron oxide. Fire to 1280°C–1300°C with a heavy reduction.

Don't forget that the clay body will have a marked effect on the fired result of the glaze. The clay that Jim has used is high in both iron and silica and comes from a supplier in Cornwall.

people to burn unwanted animal bones, chicken carcasses etc., if they have one of the larger stoves that may also operate a central heating system. It is my belief that small particles of bone, small enough to pass through a 60's sieve, can cause blistering in the glaze. I include this piece of information, not as fact but as a suspicion, having experienced the problem and eradicated it by taking a number of steps, one of which was to ensure that bone material is never put into our burner. It's worth mentioning here also that we never burn any material of a synthetic nature e.g. cellophane wrappings, plastics

Covered jar 15" high by Thomas & Constance Clarkson.
Thomas and Constance Clarkson are from Charlottesville, Virginia and work as a team, each contributing to every piece that they make.
The ash for their glazes comes from the wood-burning stoves that heat their house and is a mix of hardwoods but mostly hickory and oak. The Clarksons choose **not** to wash their ash; it is screened through a large mesh to remove the larger pieces of debris and then mixed directly into the glaze batch approximately two weeks before it is required.
This jar has been covered in a porcelain slip which was then textured and then glazed with:

Ash	50
Ball clay	20
Potash feldspar	30

The ball clay should contain as little iron as possible. Colouring oxides were then sprayed on top of the glaze.
The combination of the textured porcelain and the running ash glaze has created a rich surface quality.

etc. But, unlike Hamada, I am not so purist that we exclude papers, particularly newspaper. This must inevitably mean the introduction of a fractional quantity of clay but it really doesn't alter the quality of the ash in any appreciable way.

The agricultural community can be providers of ash in a number of ways. Farmers often need to cut back the trees and bushes around their fields, sometimes extensively, so that they can weave the remaining branches into a new neat hedge. This is, in the main, a winter or early spring activity, the quiet time on the farm while waiting for the frantic weeks of the lambing season, and it results in a series of bonfires of all the prunings along the length of the hedge. This ash is usually a cocktail of different hedgerow trees; hawthorn, hazel and ash are the most common in our area. Having obtained the permission of the farmer, simply scoop up the ash into a bag and take it away.

One word of caution, and this applies to the gathering of ash from any fire laid on the earth as opposed to concrete. Be careful not to gather up any soil or calcined gravel. The iron from these will contaminate the ash and eventually produce colours not necessarily typical of the ash you've been so careful to locate.

Farmers also burn off the stubble from their fields. The ash from cereal crops has a particular quality. As you will see from the table on page 26 they are very high in silica. I have in the past used straw ash as a substitute for quartz. Cardew (in *Pioneer Pottery*) suggests this in a pioneering situation and Hamada used rice husk ash in a number of his glazes, particularly in the glaze called Nuka. This glaze has been reconstituted in the West where rice is a far less common crop, using quartz or flint as an almost direct substitute. Stubble burnings are, I'm afraid, very difficult to gather as they lie so thinly on the soil. Farmers do from time to time burn old bales of hay that may have developed mould, but be careful not to confuse hay with straw. Hay is a rather random mixture of grass with other meadow plants such as clover. Generally a hay ash will contain much less silica than a straw ash and have a higher alkali content which is much more similar to a typical wood ash than the ash of most cereal crops. It is worth mentioning that while the average wood ash only represents approximately 1%, at best, of the original weight of dry wood, hay can produce up to 8% of its weight as ash. (See the reference to straw ash in the following photograph caption.)

This small bowl is glazed with straw ash only. Straw ash is peculiar in that it contains within itself a balance of silica with the alkaline fluxing oxides so as to become a natural glaze.

In practical terms the straw ash would require an addition of alumina, in the form of clay, to overcome the tendency to run but, unlike a pure wood ash, we already have a smooth, glassy covering that doesn't show any sign of the corrosive nature that we see in colour test 9, p. 82.

The ash on the test tile has quite clearly formed itself into a textured surface, the straw sample has remained a flat, smooth glass.

If you live in a rural area, local newspapers can be an excellent source of information. A potter friend of mine recently noticed a front page report in his local paper. It concerned the burning down of a barn containing many tons of hay. He went along and asked the farmer for access and came away with ten fertilizer sacks full of grass ash.

Large orchards, with their rows upon rows of fruit trees, like those in Herefordshire and Somerset, can provide ash. Most years some, if not all, of the trees are pruned back and the prunings are burnt in large bonfires on frosty nights in early spring to protect the blossoming trees from the cold.

Another source worthy of investigation is the large estates and country parks which accompany our large stately homes. Try and talk to the gardeners especially in the autumn when pruning takes place. The wood ash you may obtain here is likely to be a mixture, most probably of hardwoods. I recently obtained a quantity of rhododendron ash by following this selfsame line of enquiry.

I have one particularly interesting source of hardwood ash which is a fine example of the old adage, waste not want not. A lady who lives quite close to me is a paper maker. Part of the process of paper making requires a strong alkaline solution which I believe acts as a mordant in the dyeing process. After some experimentation this lady has discovered that the liquor that remains after washing a quantity of wood ash is perfect for her purpose. So, after passing the water through the ash and collecting her solution, the sodden but partially washed remainder is then bagged and passed onto me needing only to be dried to be able to be used in a glaze batch. Between myself and the paper maker we have used the original wood three times and literally nothing has been wasted.

Another possible avenue worthy of investigation is the smoking industry. By that I am not suggesting that potters should be seen surreptitiously emptying the contents of ash trays. I am talking of the smoking of food. It's not so long ago that all the smoking of produce such as meat and fish was carried out with smoke from oak chips. Unfortunately, as with so many other things, modern science has taken over and the industry now uses a chemical pellet to create the smoke and a dye to simulate that golden colour. However, for anyone within striking distance of the Arbroath area there are, thankfully, a few traditional smokeries remaining where ash may be obtained along with a tasty haddock or two!

The city dweller may feel that all this is easy to say but rather more difficult in practice and I sympathise a little. However, it is interesting to note that the pine ash which forms the basis of one of my standard glazes, having been burnt in our central heating boiler, comes from a large wood yard situated on a dockside in industrial South Wales. This wood, in the form of log ends, comes free of charge. They are glad for me to remove it and far more than I can collect is taken away and dumped. I have a similar arrangement with a local sawmill where I collect offcuts for fuel for one of my kilns. They are glad to see the back of it and whilst the kiln doesn't produce any usable ash, this wood could easily be burned specifically for use as a glaze material.

If one has any serious intentions of using wood

ash glazes on any more than just a few pots then a regular source of one particular ash or a fairly constant mixture of ashes is essential. Whilst experimentation can be exciting it can also be frustrating if it takes all of a sample of ash to produce a beautiful glaze and you have none left to mix larger quantities.

The collection of ash in reasonably large quantities from places like those I have mentioned is not difficult. It just requires a little time and common sense. I am sure that there are other places that one could look that I haven't thought of, especially abroad where certain agricultural activities produce waste products that are fit only for burning. I'm thinking here possibly of certain nut productions where the shells are surplus to needs. In any event, if all your best efforts are unrewarded, there remain two ways in which you can obtain your ash: you can either burn the wood yourself or you can buy it. Most of the larger pottery supplies companies will supply wood ash although it is expensive. On the plus side, as a rule, it is fairly consistent as they take their supplies from the same place each time.

The Preparation of Ash

First the fire

As I have suggested, the burning of wood solely for the purpose of obtaining the ash for glaze making can be a frustrating business. It first of all depends on having a fairly large quantity of wood to start with if you intend anything more than some experiments followed by the glazing of a few pots. I would suggest that a half ton of wood should provide a quantity worth persevering with.

It is interesting to note that Emil Wolff in his work with ash analyses at the end of the last century, discovered that there are considerable differences in the amounts of ash that different plants will render. He found that wood rarely gave more than one half of 1% of its original dry weight in ash. This means that to obtain just one pound of ash one would require 200 lbs of dry wood to begin with. These figures can be compared with the ashes from most types of grass. Oat straw for instance, was found to render 7.2% of its original dry weight as ash and as a general rule of thumb a figure of 5% of the original dry weight of organic material is left after the burning of grass.

If these figures don't deter you, then you should begin by finding a place for your fire that is free

from soil or gravel as these can contaminate your ash when you later try to scoop it up for storage. A concrete area or, as I have used, some old tin sheeting, are good alternatives.

Next you have to construct a shallow box of brick or concrete to retain your fire. To build a fire completely unprotected from the breeze would mean that too many of the finer particles would be lost and it is those finer particles that we are particularly interested in. Your box should be approximately 18 inches high; the length and width can be determined by the length of your logs. Leave some small gaps in the brickwork around the base of the walls to allow for the passage of air into the fire.

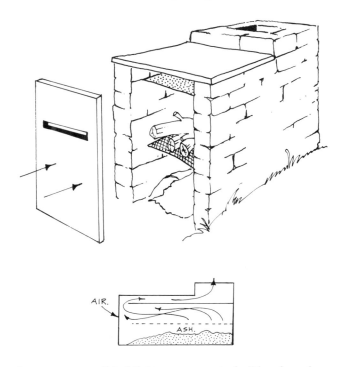

As you can see, this 'kiln' is very easy to build and can be left in situ and used as and when you have wood to burn. The lower diagram shows that the baffle (seen in the main drawing as a dotted area) completely seals the top part of the chamber apart from a small gap toward the front. Air is allowed in via the slot cut in whatever is used for the 'door'. This slot can be made bigger if the fire is too slow. The chimney can be extended either with further courses of brick or with a metal tube. I found that an old salt glaze sewer pipe worked well. I have used old kiln shelves for the top of the chamber.

The ash is removed with a shovel from the front. Since this system works it is a pity not to put the heat produced to a good purpose, so put a wood-burner in the house!

Light your fire using some newspaper if you need to. Some dried leaves would probably suit the purist better, but don't use small sticks of another type of wood if you wish to keep your ash pure. Develop a good hot fire with the smaller pieces of wood before adding the larger logs. This will help them to burn. Obviously the ideal conditions for burning would be a breezy day but this would mean losing a lot of the fine ash to the wind, so choose a still day preferably in winter or early spring during periods of low pressure when there is less updraught.

You will need to stir the fire from time to time to allow air to reach underneath. If this isn't done, large amounts of the wood will remain as charcoal. Stir gently though, or again you will lose that precious fine ash. A large fire may take up to three days to burn through completely but when all is burnt, cover the burning box with some old sheeting and allow to cool. This may take a day or two as ash has excellent insulating properties. On another still day carefully scoop up the ash, which by now should be a pale grey or pinkish powder, and store it in whatever you have available. An old plastic lidded bucket is ideal although I use polythene fertilizer sacks. Your ash is now ready for the next step in the procedure.

(The above method for burning wood to ash was that advocated by Katherine Pleydell-Bouverie and later reinforced and improved upon by Eric James Mellon in an article in *Ceramic Review* in 1976.)

Recently I have had a wood burning stove installed in the living room and I immediately noticed how efficient this machine is at turning wood into a pure white, very light, fluffy ash with little or no charcoal. It occurred to me that a cruder version of this stove could easily be built out of doors using bricks and some old tin sheeting.

The basic principle of the stove is to burn the wood slowly but thoroughly without the presence of air underneath the fire. Air is allowed into the stove over the fire and then the hot gases are persuaded to linger inside by the insertion of a baffle in front of the flue exit. As can be seen from the diagrams on p. 34, I built the structure using ordinary reclaimed housebricks. The hearth can be created from chicken wire or any sort of mesh which will allow the ash to fall through. I used metal rods set into the clay and sand mortar at 1 inch intervals. I wasn't sure whether the baffle had any real effect on the burning of the wood although it occurred to me that if it slowed down the exit of the hot gases this might in turn slow down the fire so I included it anyway. I made the roof from some old kiln shelves and sealed it along the edges with the same clay and sand mix, approximately 50/50, that I had used for

the mortar. The front of the 'kiln' provided the only real problem in that it had to be replaceable so as to provide an entry point for the wood and yet a reasonably good fit to prevent the entry of too much air. I solved the problem with a sheet of ceramic fibreboard which is light and easily lifted in and out. I am sure there are other answers, just try and use what you have lying around.

The 'kiln' worked perfectly. A much slower burn produced a similar ash to that from the indoor stove although it did require more attention in that stoking was needed more frequently. The obvious advantage, apart from a superior quality ash, is the complete protection from the elements.

Ash Contamination

Referring back, just for a moment, to the point I made earlier about the contamination of wood ash during the processing. It is important to realise that even a small amount of soil or gravel can be a major influence on the ash sample. As I have said earlier, only approximately 0.5% of the original wood remains as ash after burning. Let's assume for the moment that we are using a wood that has been felled and sawn up on site. It is fairly safe to assume that the trunk hit the ground with a considerable impact and the branches were sawn and dragged along the surface and possibly left on the ground

These two bowls each have the same basic glaze made with beech ash. The difference between them is that the bowl on the right was glazed with an ash glaze that was contaminated with soil equivalent in weight to 50% of the ash content. It is evident that the right hand bowl is now darker in colour than the left due to the iron content of the soil and, although it is not easy to see in the photograph, the glaze was slightly less fluid.

This type of contamination may not prove a problem if you are working with ash glazes that contain, for instance, red clays where the small iron content of the soil would easily become overpowered. However, if you wish to produce light or off-white glazes then contamination should be something to watch out for.

for a time where they may have been splashed with mud. Depending on how rough the bark was and how damp the conditions were at the time, it is perfectly possible for the bark to collect 0.5% of the total weight of the wood as soil during the felling process. As the mineral content of the soil remains during the burning of the wood and we burn away only the vegetable matter (let's assume that is 50% of the total weight of the soil), we can now see that the contaminant is equal in weight to 50% of the remaining ash. In his book on the same subject, Robert Tichane provides us with the following table:

	Earth's Crust	Oak Ash	50/50 Ash and Soil
Silica	60%	2%	31%
Alumina	15%	–	7%
Potash	3%	10%	6%
Soda	3%	1%	2%
Lime	5%	72%	36%
Magnesia	4%	–	3%
Iron oxide	6%	0.6%	3.5%
Titania	1%	–	0.5%
Phosphate	0.3%	6%	3%

From the figures in the final column we can see that the ash sample has changed its character enormously. From the highly alkaline substance as pure oak ash we now have an almost neutral, glaze-like material.

Contamination can take place at other times. We have already mentioned the surface on which wood is burned as a possible source but we also have to consider that wood burnt in a cast iron or sheet metal stove may contain extra iron from the inside surface of the combustion chamber. Old wood may contain nails or screws. One of my students who, after being with us one summer, went home and began using wood ash glazes based upon my recipes, found that every time she used one particular glaze, instead of the expected bottle green celadon, she obtained the most stunning blood red. This was a mystery to her and to me until I discovered that a small portion of the wood that was burned to create the ash was old timber reclaimed from a roof renovation and it still retained some of the old electrical wiring which, of course, supplied the copper oxide which in turn provided the red glaze – a careless but fortuitous accident.

Eric James Mellon has discovered a source of contamination that may well have confused a less observant potter. Eric lives near the coast and has discovered that trees that he has burned contain a fine silica sand. This, he says, has been embedded in the wood of the trees by the prevailing winds. This sand is fine enough to pass through a 60's sieve and it radically alters the balance of the ash.

I am not suggesting that we should wash wood before we burn it, although this may prove a necessity on occasions. However, we should be aware of the potential of certain situations for contamination so that any eventual unexpected variation can possibly be accounted for.

Washing of Ash

Should it be washed or not?

Having obtained our ash we now have a decision to make, do we wash it or use it as it comes? It seems that there are potters who do both, so, does it really matter?

All plant ashes contain soluble compounds: potash, carbonates, sulphates and chlorides. A certain amount of these soluble alkalis has to be removed otherwise they can cause problems later on when the ash is part of a glaze batch. They can be detected in the glaze slop as a soapy softness in the water and by smell. Anyone who has bought a recently stripped piece of pine furniture will recognise the odour of caustic soda.

YOU SHOULD NEVER STIR AN ASH GLAZE WITH YOUR HANDS.

In most instances water that has been steeped in ash becomes caustic and can burn the skin or at least cause irritation and soreness. The ash dust is also caustic and every effort should be made to prevent the breathing in of the dust when either gathering the ash or when weighing it out and sieving. A rubber mask should be worn, the type with a detachable throwaway filter, not the one-piece paper type which I have found wholly ineffective.

The removal of these soluble alkali compounds is a double-edged sword. On the one hand, if we don't they can cause the phenomenon known as deflocculation in the glaze bin, a real nuisance that can render a glaze unusable. On the other, as we remove them the ash becomes increasingly refractory and it is possible to lose as much as 25% of the fluxing power of your ash in washing. The effect of deflocculation is to impart to the fine particles that are held in suspension in the glaze slop a similar electrostatic charge. In this state they repel one another and are unable to gather together in close proximity. The net effect of this is to provide a glaze slop that appears to be of the right consistency for dipping but that in actual fact contains far too much water. Any pot dipped into a glaze in this state shows a very thick coating which is largely water. As the coating dries, usually very unevenly, we are left with a glaze layer far too thin to be of any use. I have experienced this problem in a minor way with a number of different ashes and have been able to cure it with the washing procedure I am about to describe. On one occasion however, the problem was such that I was unable to eradicate it at all. A particular batch of oak ash was at fault. It contained so much soluble alkali that the ash deflocculated in the washing bin long before the other materials for the glaze were added to it. This proves two things: first, that it isn't only clay particles that deflocculate and that wood ash must contain particles of colloidal size for deflocculation to take place at all. In theory one should be able to reverse the process by the addition of an acid (say, calcium chloride or vinegar) to the glaze slop. However, in my experience, once this reaction has taken place to all intent and purpose it is irreversible. The resulting acidic balance of the solution only encourages more alkali into solution and the sequence begins again.

The soluble alkali salts held within a wood ash contribute to the fluxing action of the ash within the glaze. It isn't possible to remove all the solubles by washing and those that remain in a much weaker concentration do no harm to the slop. As the pot is dipped into the glaze the solubles are taken into the body of the pottery and a small amount remains there which helps to flux the body-glaze layer. If the water contained in your ash glaze slop is very alkaline, as it can be, especially in the case of glaze slops made with unwashed or only partially washed ash, then the penetration of these alkalines into the body can have serious effects. It is possible to flux the body to an extent where distortion and slumping may occur. I have to say that I have never experienced this problem but then I wash my ash thoroughly. I can imagine though, that pots with a particularly thin wall section could be at risk. Larger pieces with a correspondingly thicker wall should never present problems. I have a motto that says 'a problem isn't a problem until it occurs' and on that basis I haven't worried unduly.

A certain amount of the solubles migrate to the surface of the glaze during the drying and crystal-

lize there. During the firing these compounds enter into and promote glaze melt. There are potters who contend that it is best not to wash the ash at all. That to wash away the fluxes is to rob the ash of much of its inherent qualities and fluxing ability. I feel that on balance washing is a good idea. For the potter making larger pieces of, perhaps, a more sculptural nature where he may feel that mixing a glaze batch can be specific to a pot and he doesn't need to keep quantities of glaze for lengthy periods, then O.K. For a potter like myself who requires an element of consistency and the convenience of storing glaze batches from one firing to the next, then at least an element of washing has to take place. I am not at all sure that ash glaze slops mixed from unwashed ash would keep in the bucket for more than a few weeks or in some cases days before deflocculation sets in. My advice is to always wash your ash and this is how to set about the task.

This tile shows two samples of the same batch of elm ash, one washed and the other unwashed. There is really very little difference in the fired quality of the two samples. The unwashed ash has a 'halo' of discoloration in the surrounding clay area, evidence of a greater concentration of alkaline oxides which have volatilised and 'vapour glazed' the clay.

I cannot wholly account for the difference in colour between the two samples. I can only guess that the unwashed ash, being a stronger alkaline material, has bleached the iron from itself and the body, and the iron was carried away with the volatile potassium and soda.

From these two samples it is a reasonable assumption that a moderate washing of the ash will not have any significant effect on its action in the glaze but may well prevent other problems in the glaze slop (see text).

How to wash your ash

You will require a large plastic dustbin or something similar. Place your ash into this but don't fill it more than halfway. Try to do this on a calm day. I can't repeat often enough how important it is to retain the very finest particles of ash. If this operation can be carried out indoors wearing a mask then so much the better. Next add water, almost to the top of the bin. Here I should explain why it is important not to fill the bin more than half full with the ash. During the first washing I have found it advantageous not to allow too great a concentration of soluble alkali to build up in the water. I have found particularly with oak ash, that this can lead to an irreversible deflocculation in the washing bin. The ash just will not settle in the water to allow for decantation. This situation means that the ash is now almost impossible to wash thoroughly and will inevitably lead to problems later on in the glaze slop.

Having added the water give the mixture a good stir and leave overnight. The following day the ash should have settled leaving a depth of yellowish discoloured water. This water will feel soapy to the touch and will have a distinct odour, nothing very pungent, but a definite smell that is easily recognisable. Remove any pieces of charcoal that remain floating on the surface, stir once more and allow to settle back. Then carefully pour off the water, so as not to stir up the settled ash. This may be more easily achieved by a syphon but be careful not to take the liquid into the mouth. Now repeat the process of adding clean water up to the top of the bin but this time you can leave the whole lot to soak for two or three days. Again, pour off the water without disturbing the ash. This time it should feel less soapy and some of the odour will have disappeared. It now remains to repeat these steps until the ash is washed enough for your particular needs.

1 This is how wood ash looks as it comes from the wood-burning stove. You can see the large pieces of charcoal, but don't worry about them at this stage.

3 Carefully place the ash into the bin. Try to avoid creating dust as this will mean you are losing fine particles. Do not fill the bin more than half full of ash.

2 You will need a bin and a bucket. A standard plastic dustbin is ideal because of the need to use quite a large amount of water.

4 The ash in the bin.

5 Now slowly add the water until you have doubled the volume in the bin. You must add plenty of water so as to avoid the resulting alkaline liquor becoming too concentrated and thus risking deflocculation. Add the water slowly to avoid creating too much dust.

6 Give the whole lot a really good stir and then set it aside overnight to settle down.

7 The following day the charcoal, which by now has floated to the top, can be lifted off. I use an old colander for this purpose. (I keep some of the charcoal for use on the barbecue!)

8 Allow the ash to settle again. This may only take an hour or two. Then pour off the water. Having done this you can top up with fresh water and repeat the process twice more over a period of a week or so. This time factor isn't crucial. I have sometimes left ash soaking for months

9 When you are happy that the ash is washed enough (2 to 3 washings), pour off the water for the last time, being careful not to lose any ash in the process. You are now left with a thick, lumpy slurry. Ladle this slurry into some old and unwanted biscuit fired bowls and set them aside to dry. I leave them outside on a wooden pallet covered with some galvanised sheeting that allows air to circulate around them. Drying time depends heavily on the weather.

10 Here you can see that the bowl of ash wood ash on the left has dried and is ready to be stored.

Katherine Pleydell-Bouverie and Bernard Leach both insisted that the water that remains should be clear, colourless and practically odourless. In practice this is almost an impossibility where calcium oxide is present. Most ashes will contain amounts of calcium in a hydrated form. Calcium hydroxide has only a limited solubility in water and enters into solution slowly over a prolonged period. As it takes only small amounts of this high alkaline substance to turn any slurry alkaline, one could be washing an ash sample indefinitely and still not remove all the alkali. Tichane, in his *Ash Glazes*, shows us that, in experiments carried out to discover the amounts as percentages of the total ash batch that are washed out, the initial washing, if done with copious amounts of water removes the lion's share of the solubles. Any subsequent washing removes only greatly reduced fractions.

As with most aspects of ceramics there are no rules governing when the ash is washed sufficiently well. As a guide I would say that four or five washings over a period of two to three weeks are fine. You may find that some woods require more. I have certainly found this to be true in the case of oak wood for instance. Other plants, particularly those very quick growing such as the grasses, nettles or cereal crops, may require much less or indeed none at all. It is also true that these guidelines, for that is what they are, may not suit all potters. You may find that you prefer to use the ash unwashed if this produces the qualities that you find the most attractive. Alternatively you may find that a limited washing will suffice. Should you decide on either of the latter, my advice is only to mix small quantities of glaze batch, enough to glaze those pots you have at the time. If you try to keep quantities of glaze over an extended period you may find the glaze will have deflocculated and

spoiled by the next time you come to use it. It is also possible for an ash glaze to alter its character after an extended shelf life. This is because the soluble alkalis carry on entering into solution and are therefore not so readily available as a solid to assist the glaze melt.

Drying the ash

Before the ash can be incorporated into a glaze recipe it has to be dried to facilitate accurate weighing.

The last time that you decant the water off the top of the ash in the washing bin, you are left with a thick slurry. I have found that the best way to contain the ash and still allow it to dry is to ladle the slurry into biscuited bowls that for whatever reason are no longer required. The porosity of the pottery bowls allows the passage of water through to the outside surface where it is evaporated away much in the manner of the earthenware water coolers of North Africa. I store these bowls outside but under cover which allows for the passage of air around and over the top surfaces. The speed at which the slurry dries is, of course, dependent on the weather and atmospheric moisture – in winter this can take for ever! To speed things up you can dry them over the kiln but not, as I once did, on the kiln. I learnt an expensive lesson some years ago when still using the electric kiln for biscuit firing. Having dried some bowls of ash placed directly on top of the kiln, I found, to my dismay, that the liquid had passed through the body of the pot and gathered underneath, between the bowl and the kiln's metal casing. Here, being a caustic solution, it had stripped away the paint and the zinc galvanising layer and begun to work away at the steel sheet itself. If you do use the residual warmth of the kiln to dry your ash then you will need to construct a slatted shelf over the kiln on which to place the bowls. This will need to be made of metal to avoid any risk of fire, Dexion (a prefabricated metal framework) probably being the obvious answer. Remember too, that the bowls can drip so be prepared to place a receptacle in the right place just in case.

Once the ash is dry it can be removed from the bowls into whatever you use for permanent storage. I use a large plastic bin with a tight fitting lid for the ash that I use in greatest quantity. Other smaller amounts I keep in old fertilizer sacks each clearly marked by species in indelible marker.

A Short Cut

Should you require your ash a little quicker, for an imminent firing or a pressing order perhaps, I have discovered a method that allows for the washing of the ash but doesn't require you to dry it out again before addition to the glaze. The procedure only requires some forward planning.

You wash your ash as normal but in this instance you weigh out the required quantity for the glaze batch before washing and wash only that amount. Let's say that the particular recipe that you have calls for 4000 g of ash to provide the required amount of slop. Weigh this amount from the ash as it comes from the stove or fire and carry out the procedure for washing in exactly the same way as previously described. **Make sure that you note down somewhere the amount weighed out; never trust anything to memory** (another lesson learnt early on). After washing, you need only to add the other materials in the way described on pp. 54–57, thus omitting the long drying stage if and when you need to.

Glazes, what are they and how do they work?

Essentially, glaze is a layer of glass fused to the surface of pottery. It can provide a smooth, hygienic surface that is non-porous whilst at the same time being decorative. A glaze also has the effect of strengthening the ware by the creation of a glaze-body layer. Initially this glaze is applied to the ware by various methods in the form of a powder that melts to a glass by the application of heat. In order that the ware should emerge from the kiln 'glazed' this powder should contain sufficient glass-forming oxides, of which silica is by far the most important, and the required amount of alkaline fluxes in order to fuse the silica. A glaze also requires a stabiliser, alumina. This material acts as a link between the silica and the alkaline fluxes to create a stable glass.

My own approach to glaze making is one of 'try it and see' based upon an understanding of how different materials will alter the character of a given glaze. This understanding has developed over a long period of sustained experimentation and maintaining, from batch to batch, a consistent fired result from the three or four glazes that I use most often. However, an understanding of at least the basic mechanics of what is a glaze, what is it composed of and why it melts is essential to providing a platform from which to work.

As we already know, wood ash will melt to a glass all by itself if heated to a high enough temperature. This glass is seldom of any practical use although it may have great value aesthetically. To change the character of the ash glass and with it create a glaze that is both beautiful and practical at the same time, other materials need to be added to the ash to modify it.

The Other Materials

Most of the materials used in glaze making are derived from common rocks and minerals and nearly all are hugely abundant and easily found. It is a mistake to think of glazes being made from rare or expensive minerals. The cost of a material nearly always reflects the expense of mining, preparation, refining and carriage rather than any intrinsic value of the material itself.

The names of the rocks that I speak of will all be familiar to those who have worked with glazes in any way at all — feldspar, quartz, flint, etc. However, it is important to understand that each of these materials is composed of oxides and it is the oxides that we are really dealing with in glaze making. The rocks and minerals we use are merely convenient sources of the required oxides that will achieve a certain glaze melt. Since the term, oxide, crops up so often in pottery it is as well that we should have an understanding of its meaning.

An oxide can be defined as the combination of any element with oxygen. We are all familiar with oxidation, it's around us every day. My car is oxidising at this very moment which accounts for the holes all along the bottom of the door — better known to us, of course, as rusting. The action of burning coal or wood is an oxidising process: the carbon in the fuel combines with the oxygen in the air to form carbon dioxide, the chemical reaction resulting in light and heat. The ash that is left consists of material that was already in oxide form and so did not take part in the reaction.

Throughout geological time most of the elements on the surface of the Earth have entered into combination with oxygen. Of all the oxides contained within the Earth's crust silicon dioxide or silica (SiO_2) as it is known is the most abundant and accounts for almost 60% of the total. Alumina accounts for a further 15% and all the others the remaining 25%.

Silica is the only oxide which is indispensable in glaze making. It is the main glass former and all the other oxides with the exception of alumina, can be thought of as fluxes. Their purpose in the glaze being to bring down the melting point of the silica to a more manageable level.

In the following descriptions of the raw materials I have included the chemical analyses for each one. This will tell you which oxides each of the minerals listed contributes to the glaze. Whilst it is not essential to know the oxide constituents of a mineral when using it empirically, it will certainly help you to develop an understanding of the behaviour of a mineral as a whole if there exists a knowledge of its constituent parts. *Note:* Glaze materials are supplied and used in the form of very finely ground powders. The refining and subsequent grinding render them all visually very similar in appearance and it is important that containers are well labelled so that there is no possibility of materials being confused and mixed together.

Quartz and Flint. SiO₂

As far as the potter is concerned, both of these substances can be regarded as pure silica although in theory this is only strictly true of quartz. Flint usually contains up to 4% of calcia within its crystalline structure which causes it to melt fractionally earlier than quartz but to all intent and purpose they are the same. As we have said, silica is fundamental not just to glaze making, but to ceramics as a whole and, as we shall see, occurs in many other materials including wood ash in varying amounts. Rice husk ash is almost pure silica and can just about be thought of as an impure substitute (if you can get any!). Silica of vegetable origin behaves rather differently to the naturally occurring material. The extremely fine particle size and its intimate combination with the other oxides produce a lower melting point and the ability to flux itself.

Commercially, both quartz and flint are supplied as finely ground powders. Flint is calcined before grinding; quartz, with its larger crystal structure can be raw crushed and then ground. I always use quartz for the simple reason that it is considerably cheaper than flint.

Feldspar

This is really a generic term for a group of minerals which contain silica and alumina combined with alkalis in differing proportions. Whilst the alkalis potash and soda are generally soluble, as we have already seen with wood ash, they appear in feldspars as almost insoluble. Therefore feldspars can be regarded as naturally occurring frits.

There are twelve different types of true feldspar but only two are commonly used by the potter. Orthoclase or potash feldspar which has the chemical formula $K_2O.Al_2O_3.6SiO_2$ is the most popular and where a recipe calls for feldspar but doesn't specify which one, this is the one to use. Albite or soda feldspar $Na_2O.Al_2O_3.6SiO_2$ is the other. These two are often interchangeable with very little noticeable difference. However, soda feldspar has a slightly lower melting point, due to its soda content, and begins to volatilise at 1200°C. Potash feldspar has no upper limit and is therefore found more generally useful.

Feldspars are without doubt the most important minerals available to the stoneware potter. They begin to melt at about 1150°C and because of their high alumina content do not run, even at 1300°C. Glazes can contain feldspar in very large proportions, up to 100% in theory, although additions of further fluxes are required on a practical level. Simple combinations of feldspar with wood ash, whiting, talc or dolomite in ratio of about 85:15 fired at 1300°C or so can produce beautiful glazes, although additions of a binder, such as clay, will help the glaze adhere to the pot and keep the glaze in suspension in the bucket.

In the sort of wood ash celadon-type glazes that I am interested in, feldspar usually represents between 30% and 50% of the total ingredients. I tend to think of feldspar as the body of the glaze and the ash as the character. The feldspar is the stable, consistent material, the ash is the variable.

Feldspathoids

There are other materials which are classed as feldspathoids. These are minerals which are very similar to feldspar and therefore behave similarly to feldspar but are not true feldspars because chemically they are not single materials but rather cocktails with a variable composition. Cornish stone and nephaline syenite are the two most commonly used.

Cornish stone is a decomposing granite containing feldspar, mica and free quartz with potash, soda, calcia and magnesia in varying amounts. Hence the difficulty in supplying a formula. Any given formula can only be accurate for a specific sample of rock. An analysis given by Hamer in his *Potter's Dictionary* is:

SiO_2	72.92	K_2O	3.83
TiO_2	0.02	CaO	2.08
Al_2O_3	14.95	MgO	0.09
Fe_2O_3	0.05	CaF_2	1.07
Na_2O	4.13	Loss	0.86

As you can see Cornish stone has a higher silica content than feldspar and is a little harder to melt but for our purposes it can be regarded as a mixed feldspar with extra alkaline impurities. I will sometimes use Cornish stone as a portion of the feldspar in a glaze if I feel the glaze is too runny.

Nephaline syenite ($K_2O.3Na_2O.4Al_2O_3.9SiO_2$) is a feldspathic material with an unusually high amount of soda and potassium in relation to its silica and alumina content. The resulting lower melting point of the material makes it a useful substitute for potash feldspar if one is trying to reduce the melting point of a glaze. I find, with wood ash glazes, that they really need the high temperature range 1280°C–1300°C to realise their full potential and therefore nephaline seldom appears in my recipes.

Clay

The type and amount of clay that you will need in your recipe will depend on the type of glaze that you require.

Additions of clay to a glaze will result in practical advantages even before we begin to consider any effects that it may have on the fired quality of the glaze. A percentage of clay in the batch recipe will aid the suspension of the particles in the water and help to prevent the annoying habit of some glazes, particularly feldspathic glazes, of settling brick hard in the bottom of the tub. Clay in a glaze also increases the dry strength of the unfired glaze coating thus lessening the risk of damage from chipping while on its journey to the kiln. You will also find that glazes that contain little or no clay at all are difficult to dip smoothly and have poor adherence to the pot.

Clay is essentially silica and alumina with small amounts of other elements such as calcium and iron in varying proportions depending on where the clay was laid down and the nature of the parent rocks. Silica, as we know, is the glass former but the high percentage of alumina means that additions of clay to a glaze will render the glaze increasingly more opaque while at the same time increasing the viscosity of the melt. So an obvious cure for a glaze that is running off the pot is to increase the clay content. In the celadon-type wood ash glazes which, because of a basic lack of silica, are prone to running, this stiffening property is particularly useful. It does, however, mean that the glaze can become too matt and so little movement of the glaze takes place that the result is flat and boring.

When the right balance of alumina with the fluxes is achieved the glaze takes on that quality which I most seek in a wood ash celadon, a combination of shiny, glassy areas with areas that show a crystalline structure at the surface which we call devitrification.

Clays are chemically similar to glazes but the alkali flux content of clay isn't sufficient to coax the silica content into melting. This brings us back to the ancient Chinese glazes which were simple mixtures of body clay and wood ash. The wood ash or, as in later glazes, the limestone, provided the extra fluxes necessary to form the glaze. It is as well to check the analysis of the clay you are proposing to use. What can appear on paper to be only a small difference in the silica content of a ball clay, for instance, can make a great deal of difference to the finished product. When a recipe specifies only 'Ball Clay' it may be necessary to try a number of different ball clays to discover the one that works best for the particular recipe.

Apart from any effects that additions of clay may have on the surface quality, such as stiffness and opacity of a glaze, it can also have a marked effect on the colour of the fired glaze. For the most part I tend to use China clay in my recipes. This is because it has very little iron content and I want to influence the naturally occurring colour of the ash as little as possible. Some ball clays and all the red earthenware-type clays contain quantities of iron that may range from 1% up to as much as 10% and will therefore colour a glaze accordingly. I tend to prefer the lighter tonal range and so steer away from these iron rich clays. If however, the darker range is what interests you there are all sorts of possibilities open, not only by buying prepared clays, but by digging your own local clays or collecting estuarine muds and silts. Many of these are glazes in themselves, particularly estuarine muds, and only require small additions of further fluxes such as wood ash or whiting to make perfectly usable, if often a little dull, tenmoku-type glazes.

A faceted bottle by the Author, 12" high.

This bottle was thrown to a point only just past the shoulder when it was put aside to become leather hard. The neck was then added and faceted as part of the throwing process. The sides were then immediately cut with a small cheese cutter that incorporates a guide roller to ensure an even cut.

The glaze on the lower portion was made from a dust that I collect from my local quarry. The dust is an iron-bearing granite that will fuse to a red glaze on its own. Indeed, I also use it as a 'kaki' overdip after passing it through a 120's sieve. Ball milling, of course, would be a much better method of preparation as one would be able to use all the dust rather than just the fine particles that pass through the sieve. As a general rule, a finer particle or grain size will encourage an earlier fusion due to the greater area of the material exposed to the effects of the heat.

The glaze is as follows:

Rhayader stone (Granite dust)	70
Feldspar	10
Whiting	20
Red iron oxide	3

The glaze at the top of the bottle is my standard formula using, in this case, pine ash.

I much prefer to allow the ash to speak for itself in a glaze. I gain a great deal of satisfaction from noticing even the most subtle differences in colour from one wood ash to another. Additions of materials which contain relatively high levels of colourant drown these miracles. This is only a personal approach and one open to argument. You may find that the subtle differences from one local clay or rock to another is what eventually interests you and that's fine. What I am really saying here is that personal experiment can lead you along many paths, possibly too many! At first that's O.K. but eventually you will find that one area that interests you above all others and it is then you will begin to make real progress. Wood ashes have so many variables within themselves, it seems a pity to ignore the delights that they can provide by adulterating the glaze with ingredients that will only render the glaze less ash-like. I tend to include iron in this category although I wouldn't exclude its use altogether.

Whiting. Calcium Carbonate. CaCO$_3$

In general terms, whiting is the main source of calcia for glazes. It is an abundantly occurring mineral and those rocks which are almost pure calcium carbonate are limestone, marble and chalk. Seashells are another source, which is only common sense when one considers that limestone is the result of the laying down of countless billions of sea creatures some 600 million years ago. Cardew, in *Pioneer Pottery*, describes the procedure for processing seashells. As we are concerned with using materials that are at hand it is worth repeating. He says that any clean shells e.g. clams, mussels or cockles (potters on the Gower peninsula take note!) are a useful source of pure calcium carbonate and are often easily gathered in sufficient bulk for pottery glazes. However, they are often very hard to break up. The cure is to roast them at a low temperature, which cracks and shatters them in much the same way as 'roasting' granite will shatter it. But it must be a really low temperature (not above 550°C) or else the calcium, CaCO$_3$, becomes CaO or quicklime and is much more difficult to use.

As our primary interest, in this book, is wood ash and wood ash contains anything from 30%–60% calcia it seems obvious that we shall obtain all the calcia that we need from the ash.

A large crock by Michael Casson, 12" high.

The glaze on this crock by Michael Casson is a fine example of the kind of surface one might expect from an ash glaze that contains a high proportion of clay and therefore a surfeit of alumina. The glaze has taken on a dry, opaque character which will highlight edges and is therefore particularly suited to sculptural work. It also serves well to illustrate the effects of the body clay on the glaze particularly in a reduction firing. The body here is red burning and based on fireclay. The incised lines have been inlaid with porcelain and the whole pot then dipped into a white slip of:

Ball clay	50
China clay	50

and then areas of the slip were wiped away when still wet. The pot was then dipped into a glaze of:

Ash	50	
SMD ball clay	25	
China clay	25	1280°C

The lighter areas are where the slip remained under the glaze. The dark, toasted red areas show the influence of the body clay. The ash in the glaze was acacia and unwashed.

Materials Used in Lesser Amounts

Of the other minerals available to the potter I tend to use very few in my wood ash glazes. I shall, though, run through those that I do use from time to time and their purpose although I have to admit that at least one is included in one of my standard glazes more by habit than anything else. I learnt some years ago when I played poker regularly that you don't change a winning hand!

Dolomite. $CaMg(CO_3)$

As can be seen from the formula, dolomite is calcium and magnesium together in a single crystal structure. Where calcium and magnesium are concerned a fluxing action would be expected and this is the case, in small percentages, at a high temperature. In larger quantities there is a crystalline development on cooling which produced the Dolomite matt glazes so popular in the 1960s and early 1970s. I included it, for its fluxing properties, in a glaze that I developed some years ago. I cannot be sure, but I am convinced that, as a side-effect of its inclusion, a glaze texturally similar to others I have used with pine ash, fired to a much lighter, bluer green rather than the bottle green I have come to expect from pine.

This the sort of hunch that one tends to live with for years only to find later that there was some other cause previously unthought of!

Talc. Magnesium Silicate. $3MgO. 4SiO_2. H_2O$

I have experimented with small amounts of talc in ash glazes and found it of limited value for the type of glazes that I use. Its action is to promote a mattness or buttery texture in other stoneware glazes. In my glazes it prevented the movement of the glaze and the end result became a little boring. However, I can see potential in its use if the idea is to produce an even glaze coat without the opacity derived from the use of clay.

Bone Ash. Calcium Phosphate. $4Ca_2(PO_4).2CaCO_3$

I have in the past achieved chun effects in wood ash glazes with small additions of bone ash. Bone ash contains phosphorus pentoxide in quite large proportions, maybe 44%, and it is this material which induces opacity and opalescence. Many of the old Chinese glazes, particularly the glazes on the Jun wares of the Sung Dynasty, are known to contain phosphorus although, as we have already seen, wood ash alone contains a percentage of phosphorus pentoxide and the probability is that the Chinese Jun glazes were created with an ash content.

So, wood ash, under certain circumstances, is quite capable of producing the chun effect on its own but sometimes needs a helping hand with a small addition of bone ash, say 2%–5%.

The colouring oxides

I mentioned earlier that I prefer not to use colouring oxides in my wood ash glazes as I much prefer to accept the colours and tones that the ashes give me either in their reaction with the body clay underneath or with a slip coating. If the body clay contains a percentage of iron, as mine does (about 1.5%), then the ash celadon will attract some of that iron from the body-glaze layer up into the melt thus affecting the colour. Tichane believes that the cause of this is the lime content of the ash glaze. I often use my glazes over a white slip which allows the body clay to burn through on the edges but at the same time reveals a more faithful representation of the true colour of that particular ash glaze. However, it seems to me that should one wish to influence the colour of an ash glaze then spraying an oxide mixture onto the glazed pot would be the most sensible way to proceed. One would only require a base glaze and a number of pigments to achieve endless variety. (See the photograph of Thomas Clarkson's pot on page 32.) Alternatively one could use oxide coloured slips under the glaze as in Les Miley's pot on page 51. Just to be awkward the photograph on p. 49 of a tea set by American potter Gail Russell is an ash recipe with an oxide addition to the glaze itself.

As I mentioned in the section where we discussed the use of clay in glazes, iron may be added to the ash glaze in quite large quantities by virtue of the clay used in the recipe. I somehow feel this to be a far more legitimate way of adding iron to an ash glaze rather than just simply adulterating it with the pure oxide. I realise this is probably totally illogical but it is an idiosyncrasy born out of respect for the material. 50/50 mixtures of wood ash and iron-rich earthenware or local clays will often provide interesting results.

Much depends upon the type of glaze that you wish to use as to how effective any additions of other colourants such as cobalt or copper will be. As you will see later in the book some potters create ash glazes that will accept oxide decoration either in or on the glaze. They do this by careful attention to the balance of the alumina with the other oxides within the glaze, or by increasing the silica content to a point where it is in perfect balance with its fluxes. Colours that stay bright and that do not run are the result.

Local Materials

The world around us is a huge storeroom of potters' supplies and foraging for glaze materials is not only a way of producing glazes that are, in every way, your own but the search itself is also good fun. In these days of expensive carriage charges, locally-found materials can also make sound economic sense.

In its widest sense, any thorough discussion on the subject of the gathering, processing and use of local materials would necessitate another book. However, because many of these materials are so suitable for blending with wood ashes in glaze making I shall briefly, mention where one may begin to look for useful materials and the purpose that they may serve.

Below are just a few of the possibilities. A little common sense and an inquisitive nature will, I am sure, uncover further sources of perfectly usable

materials. For my own part, I use the dust from my local quarry, a grit stone (iron-bearing granite), as the basis for a fine tenmoku and the dust from two further quarries (a granite and a limestone respectively), in a simple 85:15 mix with a small addition of quartz, to make yet another tenmoku. I make use of an iron-bearing, sandy clay from the woods above the pottery as a slip and the silt from the bed of a lake makes another. I collect a high-iron silt from a small deposit that reaches out of the bank of a small stream and I gather my own iron oxide by regularly descaling a rusty steel pipe. I have even developed some glazes that incorporate coal ash in the recipe.

In short, keep your eyes and ears open.

Eutectics

At this point it seems appropriate to discuss the principles of eutectics and the role that the eutectic point has to play in the composition of wood ash glazes. An eutectic point is the lowest temperature at which combinations of two or more substances will melt.

For example, both silica and alumina are considered highly refractory substances melting at 1710°C and 2050°C respectively. Both silica (quartz or flint) and alumina (generally incorporated into

	Materials to be found	Uses
Quarries	Granites of various type, basalt, shale, limestone, sandstone, etc.	Granites and basalts can be regarded as impure feldspars with iron. Limestone as impure whiting and shale as the clay it once was
Garden	Clay, usually red burning	Glaze and pot making
River and estuary	Estuarine silts and mud; sometimes sands and ochres, even iron oxide	Will often make good glazes on their own. Line blend with wood ash for glazes. Sand for clay bodies also slips
Farms	Clays. Wood and straw ashes	Glaze and pot making
Forestry	Wood ash. Kiln fuel	Glaze flux
Coal-fired power station	Pulverised coal ash	Glaze making
Sawmill	Wood ash and possible source of fuel for a wood-fired kiln	Glazes
Monumental mason	Granite, marble and possible slate dusts	Glaze making
Roadworks	Clay	Glazes and slips

glazes by the use of clay) are sometimes added to glazes to raise the melting point i.e. to stiffen a glaze that melts too much. However, silica and alumina have a fluxing action on each other. A 50/50 mix of these two substances melts at about 1750°C and not at the halfway point between the individual melting points as might have been expected. The eutectic mixture is 90% silica and 10% alumina which melts at 1545°C which is a point considerably lower than either individual melting points.

A porcelain teaset by Gail Russell, 9" high.
Gail Russell is married to the potter Tom Turner with whom she shares a workshop in Delaware, Ohio.
The pattern is trailed onto the leather hard pots with a porcelain slip and then glazed after a biscuit fire with:

Albany slip	44
Whiting	31
Ash	11
Ball clay	14
Cobalt carbonate	0.3

This glaze has a large percentage of whiting and there is probably scope to reduce that amount in favour of wood ash.

All the alkaline oxides exhibit a fluxing action on silica when they are intimately combined and heated. However, eutectic mixtures in glazes are not just the action of one oxide reacting with silica but a case of each oxide reacting with every other. In mixtures of more than two materials or substances made up of even larger numbers of constituents the whole area becomes progressively more complicated. As the temperature rises the simplest eutectic combinations melt first. This begins a chain reaction when the now melted glass flows only to find other combinations or oxides with which to produce further more complex eutectics.

The simple graph below illustrates, as far as the potter is concerned, the most important practical application of eutectics. The melting point of pure silica is shown at the right-hand side of the graph and diminishes as the graph moves to the left. At the left-hand side we have an imaginary alkaline oxide with its considerably lower melting point.

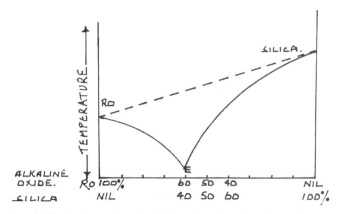

Graph illustrating eutectics. Taken from Frank and Janet Hamer's *The Potter's Dictionary of Materials and Techniques.*

Stoneware bowl, handbuilt with a wheel thrown foot. Ginny and Tom Marsh, USA.

Ginny Marsh writes: 'This pot is glazed with a mixture of 50% sieved wood ashes and 50% local red earthenware clay. We live in the "knobs" of the Southern Indiana, just north of the Ohio River. These hills are a glacial moraine eroded into the hills and valleys by the run-off melt from the glacier. While this clay and the reddish and grey rocks around all give the same result when fired, most of the creek banks are full of gravel, and the soil is more often than not a true concretion. Therefore we dig the clay from the terraces where we find deposits with very little gravel. We do the typical process of slaking the clay into slurry, sieving it and drying it for storage. The ashes are mixed hardwood from our wood burning stove. We sieve then to mesh 40, mix the glaze and sieve it again when wet.'

The alkaline oxide diminishes in amount as the graph moves to the right. Temperature is indicated in the vertical at the left-hand side. One might expect the melting points of the different combinations to fall somewhere along a straight line between the two single melting points. However, what really happens is that the melting points lie on the lower line. The lowest possible melting point, or eutectic point, is indicated E at 60% silica and 40% alkaline oxide. What is important to notice is that on the left-hand side of the graph, the increasing amount of silica, normally thought of as refractory, is having a fluxing action upon the alkaline oxide. Reading from the right-hand side of the graph it is also evident that as the silica content decreases past the eutectic point, then further increases in the alkaline oxide fraction serve no fluxing purpose at all. Indeed the opposite is true, the melting points increase.

The effect of this is sometimes noticed in glaze making when, rather against all expectations, further additions of a fluxing material such as whiting actually decrease the fusibility of a glaze, or similar additions of silica may increase fusibility.

If the end result is a clear, transparent glaze then a complete eutectic throughout all the constituent parts has taken place. If however, the process has stopped before the end point, it may be found that the glaze may contain specks of unmelted material. Hamada's Nuka glaze is a fine example of a glaze so high in silica that a portion of it cannot enter the melt. The residue, held in suspension, is the reason why the glaze appears opaque.

The ability of one material to have a fluxing effect on another is central to all glaze making. Wood ash, being already a mixture of oxides could be said, in most instances, to be a naturally occurring glaze by itself. When heated to 1280°C most wood ashes will melt to form a glass of sorts, usually mottled or streaked and yellowish in colour. Thus the theory of eutectics is shown to work as ashes contain elements with much greater melting points than 1280°C when heated alone.

The early Chinese discovered that a mixture of certain clays and lime produced a satisfactory and often beautiful glaze. The lime was introduced as wood ash or crushed or burnt limestone. Individually the three oxides involved: lime (calcium oxide), silica (silicon oxide) and alumina (aluminium oxide), have extremely high melting points but in the correct proportions, or in other words, as a eutectic mixture, they combine to form good stoneware glazes at around 1200°C. Similar glazes, using these three oxides, can be constructed using a simple mixture of China clay, quartz and wood ash or whiting. The natural impurities found in the clays and ashes used by the Eastern potters make an accurate prediction of the final melting point difficult. However, the clay-quartz-lime glaze formed the backbone of most early Chinese stoneware glazes because the required balance of oxides could be found in so many naturally occurring materials. Simple glazes of this nature can be recreated by simple combinations of clay and ash. Bernard Leach quotes a mixture of 60% siliceous clay (one of the higher silica ball clays would be ideal, possibly Hy-Plas 71) and 40% of oak ash. I have made successful glazes using a 50/50 mix of red earthenware clay and any wood or bush ash. This particular mixture works very well in oxidation to produce an Indian red mottled with ochre.

In general terms it is not necessary for the individual potter to concern himself too deeply with the highly complex chemistry of eutectics. It suffices that a basic understanding of the theory can be applied to workshop practice. The theory of eutectics is definitely the domain of the chemist. The potter can proceed in the knowledge that it happens and doesn't really need to know how, above and beyond a certain level. Simple experimentation and a try-it-and-see approach will eventually lead to an awareness and intimate working knowledge of the materials. For the potters who would like to know more I would refer them in the first instance to Frank Hamer's excellent description in *The Potter's Dictionary of Materials and Techniques*.

Making Glazes

Now we come to the most important part, the moment when all the hard, laborious work is rewarded with a beautiful glaze. I think it is true that every ash, without exception, will produce good results but, perhaps, not at the first attempt or even the second. I recently heard of a student who is achieving successful glazes by burning and then processing the ash from household rubbish. This idea isn't so absurd as it may at first seem. The rubbish would be a mixture of vegetable matter, potato peelings, etc., paper, card and so on, producing an ash that would have a reasonably consistent average content over a period of time. This story lends credence to the assertion that with a little ingenuity ashes needn't be difficult to obtain and that potters are not always environmentally unfriendly!

Testing Your Ash

It is often the case, either when starting from scratch or beginning with a new ash batch that a process of testing has to take place, initially to ascertain the inherent qualities of the ash that you have and then to decide what that ash requires in terms of additions to bring out the best from it. After many years of working with the material I have now a number of recipes that I know have worked well in the past with a variety of different ashes. The substitution of a new ash for an old, or now no longer available, ash is a good starting point, but in the first instance I will assume that we are looking at an ash that is going to be used as a material for the very first time.

A large lidded jar by Les Miley, 18" high.
This jar, entitled Wabash Contours XXIV, a title that reflects the landscape that was its inspiration, has been glazed with an ash glaze and then placed in a salt kiln. The action of the salt has been to further flux the ash glaze providing a surface of rich textural quality.

The combed pattern was made through a layer of porcelain slip that was brushed over at the leather hard stage. In reality this pot has a blue colour derived from a thin layer of slip applied to the bisqued pot prior to glazing.

Slip:	Albany slip	85
	Nephaline syenite	15
	Cobalt carbonate	2
Glaze:	Mixed ash	40
	Potash feldspar	40
	Ball clay	10

As a starting point it is a good idea to try and melt a pure ash sample on a test tile. Together with the analysis of your particular ash, if you have one, the fired tile will give you some idea of the fusibility of your ash. Place a small button of ash on a tile (perhaps, for education's sake, you may like to try samples of the ash both washed and unwashed) and fire it to the temperature and atmosphere you normally work with. It may also be interesting, if this isn't the first batch of ash you have worked with, to place on the tile, alongside the new sample, a sample of your previous ash. This may provide a useful comparison and some clues as to how to continue with your glaze. Almost without exception you will find that your ash will melt to a runny, green glass of more or less fluidity.

It would be interesting here to compare the results on the tile on page 52 with the appropriate analysis on page 139 and see whether the figures quoted in analysis and the qualities that they may suggest are borne out by the results from the kiln.

As I would have expected all the ash samples on the tile have melted to a green glass. They have been able to do this because the ash has combined with silica and alumina from the surface of the clay body to form a far more balanced glaze than would be possible if we could melt the ash totally independently under laboratory conditions. However, for our purposes there is ample information to enable us to proceed.

The sycamore and the beech are apparently very similar indeed, as are the elm and the ash. The birch is noticeably different because of the 'halo' of dark, vapour-glazing on the body surface surrounding the sample. This area also exists, to a lesser degree, around the ash and the elm but not the sycamore, beech or pine. Why? It may suggest that the bottom three ashes were either not washed samples or, at least, not so thoroughly washed as the top three. The 'halo' is evidence that there was a greater soluble flux content in those samples where the dark stain is more evident. In this case, as the ashes were placed on the tile as dry powder, the potash and soda have become volatile and glazed the surrounding area much in the same way as salt during a salt glaze firing rather than having soaked into the porous body of the clay during glazing. A comparison of the analysis of beech and birch tells me that the potassium content of beech is three times that of birch. So, bearing in mind the variability of analyses I can still safely guess that the birch sample was unwashed.

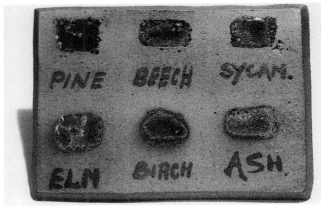

Test tile.
A 'button' test of a number of different types of ash. The tile was fired at 1280°C in a reducing atmosphere and the ash was applied in its dry powder form. For a full description of the results see text.

In other respects the fired results illustrate the less than helpful nature of ash analyses. All the samples are very similar indeed in surface quality and, with the exception of the pine, in colour. Pine is well known for its greater iron content than the hardwoods and will tend to produce glazes that are nearer to a 'bottle green' than the lighter, fresher greens from beech or elm and the like.

Having assured ourselves of the potential of our samples, let's take one of them and work our way through a pattern of tests that should result in usable glazes. For this purpose I will work with the beech sample kindly given to me by Eric James Mellon.

What Characteristics Do You Want in Your Glaze?

Initially, we have to decide what type of glaze we are looking for. When I'm asked to think about ash glazes I immediately think about the range of glazes that we know as ash celadons because this is the area that I am interested in. However, this is only one avenue of exploration. I shall endeavour to guide the reader along other paths that will result in glazes of various character. As we go along I will explain the simple logic that accompanies each progression.

First, let's deal with an ash celadon similar to that on the pot in the photograph on page 53. I have to begin by deciding on the sort of qualities that I am aiming for although, because of the nature of the material, these aims are necessarily flexible. I can't always be too exact over colour requirements for instance, but in a broad sense I can lay down certain guidelines that will dictate the nature and amounts of any further additions.

I require that my glaze should stay on the pot! This may seem obvious but where ash glazes are concerned it is a major consideration. However, I do not want the glaze so static that it becomes boring. There has to be enough movement in the glaze so that it will highlight any decoration in the clay by pooling in hollows and running away from edges. This quality in a glaze necessarily means that we are often on a knife edge between enough and too much fluidity. I do not want a glaze that is too shiny. I would prefer a surface that varies between shininess and areas of mattness. Lastly, I want a fresh, lively green colour and I won't mind if it crazes although it has to be a durable glaze. Customers returning pots that haven't survived the dishwasher won't enhance my reputation as a potter!

Taking the above information as a sort of specification it is fairly obvious that our finished glaze is going to bear the hallmarks of a typical high-lime glaze. This suggests that wood ash, being roughly 30% to 60% lime, is going to be needed in a fairly large proportion in the recipe.

Let's pause, just for a moment, and consider again what we need in the form of oxides to create a glass or glaze. As we have already seen, glass is normally thought of as a silicate and would therefore be expected to contain between 50% to 80% silica. Bearing in mind that most wood ashes contain rather small amounts of silica we can assume that we will need to add silica in quite large amounts to achieve a glassy surface. We have to remember though, that in this particular glaze the silica content need only be sufficient to form the glass. In strictly technical terms the glaze will have a silica deficiency, otherwise we would lose that special quality of movement and in doing so most of the decorative quality.

So, we have wood ash and silica in reasonable quantities. What else do we need?

We have silica and we have fluxes, but as yet we have no alumina. Alumina, as we have noted in a previous section, is the stabiliser in a glaze. It helps to prevent the glaze from running and lends body to the glass. We can, therefore think in terms of wood ash glazes of this type as additions of silica and alumina to the basic ash material, the flux.

Having decided that these are the oxide additions that we need, we now have to decide from where to obtain these oxides and in what amounts.

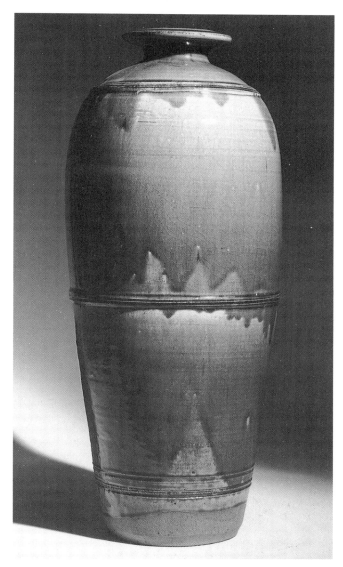

A tall bottle by Richard Batterham, 22" high.
In definitive terms a celadon is a blue or green glaze, the colour derived from firing iron oxide in a reducing atmosphere. About 3% is the maximum amount for the iron before the glaze becomes too dark to be called a celadon.

Celadons are generally thought of as fairly stiff feldspathic type glazes but I also include the more fluid green ash glazes as celadons.

This magnificent bottle is a wonderful example of the ash celadon at its sumptuous best. The depth and character of the glaze, its gentle movement and variation of tone together with a beautifully thrown and orchestrated form create a pot of immense presence.
Courtesy of Christie's Ltd.

As we know from analytical work carried out on some of the old Chinese glazes, the three oxides required to provide a perfectly good glaze, silica, alumina and calcium, can be present in combinations of just two materials. Wood ash and clay is one possibility or perhaps wood ash and a stone of some description. For our purposes here I have decided to combine wood ash, in the first instance at least, with potash feldspar which, as we already know, is a combination of silica, alumina and flux. These two materials will form the basis for the first series of tests.

At this point, we need to look briefly at the mechanics of combining our materials to create a glaze batch and, having understood this, we need to consider the different methods of blending materials for the purpose of experimentation.

Mixing the Glaze

Ash glazes are mixed pretty much in the same way as other glazes except that ash, being the rather impure and variable material that it is, requires a little special treatment. All ash, however soft or fine its quality, will always contain a percentage of its volume that will not pass through the 80's mesh sieve that I use. In addition to this, unlike some other potters using ash, I do not sieve out the larger foreign bodies, charcoal, nails, pieces of unburnt wood and the like before the washing. I did try this once while working for another potter and found it an unpleasant chore. Even with a mask and being as careful as possible, the fine dust found its way into my eyes and hair whilst providing these finer particles with another opportunity to escape. It is because the larger pieces are still in the ash that I allow 25% extra, or thereabouts depending on the ash, when weighing out. This extra percentage is expressed in the glaze recipe and in general terms never need to altered unless the solid material is sieved out at an earlier stage. You will notice later in the book that my recipes seem to contain rather large amounts of ash by comparison. This is the reason why. *Remember*, you will need to make an allowance in your batch recipe for the amount of grit that doesn't pass through the sieve. Because of this percentage of waste material, I find it a good idea to sieve the ash after it's been washed and then use it in the recipe.

My procedure for the mixing of a typical ash glaze is as follows: First, weigh out the required amount of ash calculated to provide you with the correct amount of finished glaze slop. Place this in a bucket and cover with water. Stir the mixture and break up any lumps, then allow it to stand for five or ten minutes. I find this allows the ash to become thoroughly wetted and makes for easier sieving

later on. I find that an 80's mesh sieve is generally adequate for my purposes though sometimes if an ash is particularly coarse I will use a 60's mesh. Place the sieve on two battens across the rim of an empty bucket and gently pour the slop into the sieve filling the bucket halfway. A nylon washing up brush makes an ideal lawn brush and is a lot cheaper. Use this, in a gentle, rhythmic, circular motion to coax the usable ash through the sieve.

1 Weigh out the required amount of ash that will provide the right quantity of slop for your container. Remember that to have too much glaze in a bin is almost as much of a nuisance as too little!

2 Place the ash in a container. At present it still contains unwanted charcoal, grit and other extraneous foreign bodies.

to the required density. As a rough guide the glaze should have a pint weight of around 28 ounces but ash glazes can produce markedly different finishes depending on the thickness of application. You will have to experiment to find the thickness that produces the effect you want. I find now that after many years of using this type of glaze, I can judge the right density from observing the movement of the slop while stirring it before use.

3 Now add water to the ash, perhaps twice the volume of the ash to start with.

As the level in the sieve goes down add a little more from the original bucket until the whole amount is used up. You may find that you will need to add fresh, clean water to help the process along which is perfectly all right. You will also find that you have quite a large residue remaining in the sieve. Before you discard this flush it through three or four times with clean water to make sure that you have utilised every possible grain of usable ash. Don't worry if you seem to have used far more than the required amount of water, the ash will quickly settle to allow you to decant some of it.

While the ash is settling, you can use the time to weigh out the other materials required for your glaze batch. Place these into another bucket. Add some of the water out of the bucket with the ash in it to these materials and give them a good stir. Now, using the 80's sieve or a finer one if necessary, sieve these materials into the bucket with the ash.

A really good, prolonged stir with a wooden paddle is now all that's required to render the glaze slop ready for use. If you find that there is still too much water in the bucket and the glaze is correspondingly thin, then you will need to allow the mix to settle, possibly overnight, and then decant again

4/5 Having given the ash and water mixture a good stir to thoroughly wet the ash and to break up any lumps, you can now pass the slurry through a sieve. Suspend the sieve over a second container, pour in the slurry and with a circular motion of the brush work the mixture through the 80's mesh sieve.

55

8 Pour the sieved ash and water mixture back into the original bucket now thoroughly washed out.

6/7 Keep washing the ash throughout the sieving with clean fresh water to ensure that you use all the available ash. You will be left with a residue of grit and charcoal. Throw this away.

9 Now weigh out the other materials required for your glaze recipe.

10 Decant some of the water from the sieved ash and water mixture and discard it (some potters keep it to add to the glaze during its usable lifetime as it contains some soluble fluxes). Then pour some of the ash and water mixture on to the other materials and give them a thorough stirring.

13 A good stir is now all that's required. You may find, especially if the glaze contains Cornish stone, that the whole quantity will need to be passed through the sieve again to make sure there are no small lumps. Cornish stone has a habit of rejoining itself on the other side of the sieve; a second sieving will remedy this.

Methods of Blending Materials

The line blend

The line blend is the simplest method for mixing a complete variation of two materials. It is done by increasing the amount of one material while decreasing the amount of another. This is usually achieved using a scale of 0 > 100 in increments of 10 at the top and the reverse underneath (see table on page 58).

For most practical purposes I can see little point in including samples 1 and 11 where the materials stand on their own. Indeed, when an understanding of the behaviour of the different glaze-making materials has developed, Numbers 2 and 10 can also probably be omitted. It is possible that after an initial run of tests by this method that a further series may be necessary with a smaller incremental adjustment. This is simply done but it must be remembered that the total of each individual test must be 100.

11/12 Pour this mixture into the sieve which is now suspended over the remaining ash and water mix and work through with the brush as before.

sample	1	2	3	4	5	6	7	8	9	10	11
Material A %	100	90	80	70	60	50	40	30	20	10	0
Material B %	0	10	20	30	40	50	60	70	80	90	100
Total	100	100	100	100	100	100	100	100	100	100	100

A simpler and equally effective method of testing two materials, that I call the progression method, is as follows:

First test

five parts of A + five parts of B

This is obviously a 50%/50% mixture. Dip your first test piece. Now add a further two parts of B to the existing mixture, we now have,

Second test

five parts of A + seven parts of B

Taking the total of the parts i.e. 12 and then dividing this into each individual material and then multiplying by 100 we find that this mixture represents,

A 41.5%
B 58.5% Rounded up

Dip your second test piece.

Third test

five parts of A + nine parts of B

which translates as:

A 35.5%
B 64.5% Rounded up

Dip your third test piece.

You can now continue in this fashion as many times as you wish just adding further amounts of two parts of B to the existing mixture and then resieving each time. This series will illustrate the effects of adding more and more of one material to another which remains constant. To complete the picture simply reverse the materials and repeat the series over again. I find this method particularly useful in gauging the amount of an addition to a previously mixed glaze in order to bring the glaze to a required quality.

Tri-axial blends

Blends of three materials can be worked out from a tri-axial diagram. This diagram has the form of a triangle that consists of many smaller triangles. Each point where lines meet or intersect, represents a combination of materials and is given a number. Daniel Rhodes provided the following diagram in *Clay and Glazes for the Potter* together with an accompanying explanation.

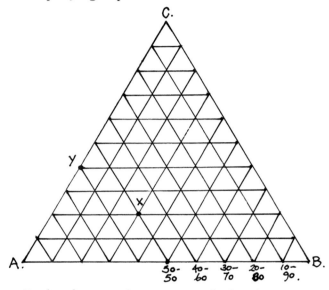

'In this diagram the points on the line between A and B and between B and C and between A and C are, in effect, the same as the line blends previously described. The mid-way point in each line represents half of one member and half of the other. Other points on the outside lines of the triangle have more or less of the end members, depending on the position of the point, each point in this case representing one tenth of the line. The composition of point Y, for example, will be 60% of A and 40% of C. The composition of a point on the inside of the tri-axial blend will depend upon its distance away from the points at the corner. Point X, for example will contain 50% of A, since it is five spaces removed from A. X will contain 30% of B, since it is seven spaces removed from B, and 20% of C, since it is eight spaces removed from C. Similarly, the composition of any other point in the diagram can be determined.'

The above plan is known as the 66-point tri-axial because there are 66 points where lines intersect. A smaller version, the 21-point plan is simply created by halving the number of sections along each side so that the increments move along in 20s rather than 10s.

The following are possible combinations for tri-axial experiments each involving wood ash:

1. Wood ash, feldspar, any clay.
2. Wood ash, local stone, feldspar.
3. Wood ash, local stone, whiting.
4. Wood ash, cornish stone, any clay.
5. Wood ash, red clay, another clay.

All three of these blending methods are particularly useful in dealing with 'found' materials when the precise chemical analysis is not known.

Test Series 1

The photograph below of the fired results of our line blend fired to 1280°C using the beech ash and potash feldspar show that, with the exception of Number 5, we have four seemingly excellent glazes of differing character.

Number 1 is a semi-opaque, off-white glaze and hasn't run at all. The iron spots are showing a lustrous red colour and the glaze would probably take iron brushwork particularly well.

1 A line blend of beech ash and potash feldspar.

Ash	15	30	45	60	75
Feldspar	85	70	55	40	25

I have used quite large increments between the figures. You may decide that you wish to increase the amounts more gradually perhaps by increments of ten up to 100.

Number 2 is beginning to show more fluidity in the glaze due to the increase in the percentage of ash and a decrease in feldspar. The colour is also greener, due in part to the increase in ash and the therefore higher iron content and partly to the increased calcia content leaching iron from the clay body into the glaze. Tichane, in his book *Ash Glazes*, calls this action 'body bleaching'. The action of calcia is to take iron from the glaze/body layer which leaves a characteristic whitening under the ash glaze and imparts a deeper green colour to the glass.

Number 3 is very similar to Number 2 except it is a little darker and slightly more fluid.

Number 4 Now we are seeing the qualities that I set out to achieve. A good green colour and just the right amount of movement. See how the glaze has gathered above the central line and in the impressed pattern.

Number 5 is showing an extreme lack of silica and alumina. There is no body to the glaze and the colour is poor.

From the test pieces, any one of Numbers 1 to 4 could be the basis for further experimentation depending on the type of glaze you are aiming to achieve. For me, Number 4 is the one to choose. It has those qualities which I look for in an ash glaze. Number 1 is a particularly fine glaze and may be just what someone else may be looking for.

If any one of the mixtures in the line blend are exactly what we are looking for or in the unlikely event that we only require one glaze to work with, then theoretically we need go no further. It is more likely, though, that because of the potter's inquisitive nature and an understandable desire to have a variety of glazes to work with, further line blends may be tried.

Colour test 1

Although, in test Number 4 we have a glaze that is perfectly usable, in general terms it is a good idea to include some clay in a glaze formula. Clay will help to suspend the glaze in the bucket and create a stronger unfired coating that is not so prone to damage prior to firing. I also find that additions of clay to ash glazes of this type help to create a variegated surface. Instead of rather a shiny covering I am looking for a surface that is matt in places becoming deeper and shinier as the glaze pools and runs creating areas of glassy movement over a matt background.

Test series two

For a second series of tests I have taken the base recipe Number 4; i.e.

Ash	60
Feldspar	40

and, by the progression method described earlier, I have, added 10 parts of China clay to the base and dipped each bowl after sieving.

Number 1 is the base glaze.

Number 2 has 10 parts of clay added and as you can see the glaze has absorbed this much clay with very little overall effect. There is still movement and the colour remains unaltered because I am using China clay. If we had used a ball clay we would expect to see a darker tone because of the added iron and slightly greater fluxing due to the small percentage of alkalines in ball clays.

Number 3 is noticeably less fluid and therefore, for me anyway, has less character.

Number 4 has no movement at all and the 30 parts of clay have rendered this a matt glaze with a pleasant satin surface but not the glaze I am looking for. What this series does tell us is that for matt glazes there will be a high clay content. See the photograph of Mick Casson's crock on page 46.

From the tests in Series 2 I am very happy with Number 2 which is:

Ash	60
Feldspar	40
China clay	10

which, expressed as a percentage is,

Ash	54.5
Feldspar	36.5
China clay	9

and it can be as simple as that!

Different feldspars or clays will give you a multitude of different results as will altering the ratio of the basic materials. We have already seen how progressive additions of clay can alter the surface quality. Colour tests 1 (on p. 59) and 2 (on p. 62) show the above glaze with, in Colour test 3 progressive additions of 10 parts of feldspar. One can see that each time a further 10 parts is added so the glaze becomes less fluid until in Number 4 we have a smooth, static celadon.

In Colour test 4 I have added further additions of 10 parts of wood ash. As the series progresses the extra fluidity is evident until we reach Number 4 and the glaze has run right off the pot!

It is only by carrying out these sorts of exercises that a full working knowledge of your materials is gained. If nothing else, the above series of tests should illustrate how simple working with ash glazes can be and how great are the margins for error. From these few simple blends we already have a number of fine glazes of differing surface qualities and colour. From here the scope is limitless.

Possible further line blends are as follows:
1. Wood ash and nepheline;
2. Wood ash and any flux (e.g. Dolomite);
3. Wood ash and Cornish stone;
4. Wood ash and any clay (including local clays);
5. Wood ash and local stone dusts;
6. Wood ash and porcelain clay.

After gaining some experience and an expanding knowledge of how the different materials behave, further combinations of materials may suggest themselves. However, within these suggestions for high-fired tests lay a number of simple and beautiful glazes that are similar to some of the earliest and best Chinese glazes of the Han, Tang, and Sung dynasties.

To try and cover the full range of possibilities of ash glazes is beyond the scope of this book. With an ever expanding understanding of the function of glaze materials your glazes can become more complex in composition as you try to achieve new and perhaps more individual glazes. You may decide, as I have, that the more simple the approach the better.

Colour test 5 is a line blend of ash with a red earthenware clay. Number 3 shows distinct possibilities but requires a further small addition of feldspar or quartz to lend a little more body to the glass.

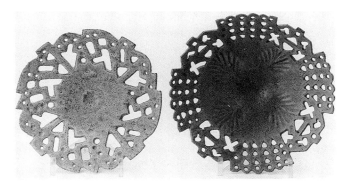

Carved and pierced plates by Ian Godfrey, 9" diameter.
These plates have been fired in an oxidising atmosphere and have an ash glaze similar to 15a in the list of glazes at the back of this book. Try using different clays or addition of colouring oxides particularly cobalt/copper mixes for various effects.
Courtesy Christies Ltd.

The line blend in Colour test 6 is of ash and the granite dust from my local quarry. There are a number of trials here that show promise. Numbers 4 to 10 are all worth pursuing. I chose to work with Number 10 which is,

Ash	10
Granite dust	90

On studying the trial closely I decided that, for a tenmoku, it wasn't quite dark enough for my taste so I added a small amount of iron oxide which would also behave as a flux. To increase the body of the glaze I incorporated 10 parts of potash feldspar. The recipe now looked like this:

Ash	9
Granite dust	80
Potash feldspar	9
Red iron oxide	1.5

The glaze had more 'body' but was rather too red and a little static. I decided that Number 9 in the line blend was more the quality of surface I was looking for so I simply increased the ash in the recipe above and the iron content accordingly. The glaze recipe was now:

Ash	20
Granite dust	72
Potash feldspar	8
Red iron oxide	2.5

This mixture proved successful as a rich, black tenmoku and can be seen on the small test piece in the photograph below and a slightly altered version

on the large bottle in the photograph on p. 45. It has since become one of my standard glazes. It is interesting to note that trial Number 11 is the pure granite stone alone. It has fired to a smooth, lustrous red and I use this stone sieved through a 120's mesh as a 'kaki' overglaze. The sieving wouldn't be necessary if the dust was ball milled as we are only interested in a fine particle size that will melt more readily. Hamada's kaki was a pure local stone that became his tenmoku with an addition of 10% of ash.

To run simple test series of the kind described requires only the very basics of equipment, scales, 80's and 100's mesh sieves, a lawn brush (I use a much cheaper plastic washing up brush), some buckets, a few small tubs (margarine or yoghurt cartons are ideal) and of course a kiln. You do not need a thorough knowledge of chemistry, indeed, in some ways that may even be a hindrance!

As an example of how one might follow through a series of tests on a previously untried material I include the following as proof that by a series of logical steps a beautiful glaze or glazes can be brought from the most unpromising of materials.

Glaze:	Rhayader stone	72
	Ash	20
	Feldspar	8
	Red iron oxide	2.5

Coal ash

In a typical year, the Central Electricity Generating Board in the UK burns around 70 million tonnes of coal at between 1400°C and 1600°C, which produces 12 million tonnes of ash. This P.F.A. (pulversided fuel ash) is chiefly made up of silica, alumina,

Colour test 2

Colour test 3

Colour test 4

iron and calcium and is around 2%–5% water soluble and, as with wood ash, this solution is alkaline. The following is a typical average analysis of P.F.A.:

SiO$_2$	Al$_2$O$_3$	MgO	Fe$_2$O$_3$	TiO$_2$	CaO	Mn	K$_2$O	P$_2$O$_5$
47%	28%	3%	8.5%	1%	3.5%	1%	3.5%	1%

+ chlorides and sulphates and trace elements

It appears that, unlike with wood ash, an analysis can be quite specific within reasonably close parameters as the material varies comparatively little from one sample to another.

If one looks at the above analysis it is immediately obvious that it is similar in its silica/alumina balance to a clay. A typical China clay will have a silica content of around 47% and 37% alumina plus much smaller amounts of titanium and the alkaline fluxes. Below is the analysis of EWVA ball clay from Watts, Blake and Bearne:

SiO$_2$	Al$_2$O$_3$	MgO	FeO	TiO$_2$	CaO	Mn	K$_2$O	Na$_2$O
48	32.6	0.3	—	0.8	0.2	—	1.8	0.3

Apart from a substantial difference in the iron content and less alkalis there is a strong similarity.

Armed with this information my first move was to try to melt some of the material on a tile. The test tile below shows the coal ash has fused to a molten, 'sticky' mass. It is nowhere near as fluid as the ash sample alongside. However, it has fused to a degree that one would expect from certain red clays or shale dusts and is therefore a promising start.

Test tile (coal ash)
The fired results of this tile tells us two things. Firstly, that coal ash contains a significant percentage of iron and secondly that coal ash is nothing like as fusible at 1280°C as wood ash, although it has begun to fuse which is a good sign. We now have to find the right balance of fluxes to coax the high proportion of silica into melting.

Colour test 5

Colour test 6

2 This is a progression test beginning on the far left with the base glaze 4 from Series 1.

Ash   60
Feldspar   40

10 parts of China clay have been progressively added to the test batch until the final trial formula is:

Ash   60
Feldspar   40
China clay 30

3 The effect of progressive additions of 10 parts of feldspar to the base glaze of:

Ash   60
Feldspar   40
China clay 10

The final glaze in the trial series is:

Ash   60
Feldspar   70
China clay 10

4 The effect of progressive additions of 10 parts of ash to the same base glaze as 3.
The final glaze in the trial series is:

Ash   90
Feldspar   40
China clay 10

5 A line blend of ash with a red earthenware clay.

Red clay	85	70	55	40	25
Ash	15	30	45	60	75

Numbers 3 and 4 show the most promise although I feel that this particular red clay may be too high in iron. Further blends of either of these two with feldspar or Cornish stone may produce workable glazes.

6 A line blend of ash with the dust from my local quarry, Rhayader stone is a type of iron-bearing granite known in the quarrying trade as gritstone. It is quarried primarily for use in the road mending industry.

Ash	100	90	80	70	60	50	40	30	20	10	0
Stone	0	10	20	30	40	50	60	70	80	90	100

The trials read from left to right, top row first. The final test of 100% Rhayader stone is far right bottow row. (See page 61.)

My next step was to try substituting the coal ash for the clay in a celadon glaze for 1280°C:

Cornish stone	25		Cornish stone	25
China clay	25	*became*	Coal ash	25
Whiting	25		Whiting	25
Quartz	25		Quartz	25

The result was excellent. A more fluid glaze of darker tone proved that the coal ash would enter into a melt without any nasty side effects such as scumming or blistering.

My main concern was to try and create a glaze that said something about the material 'coal ash'; the problem was that I wasn't sure what that was but I decided that I would know it when I saw it!

My next step was to try and flux the ash to a greater degree than the original sample on page 62. Initially I did this by carrying out a progressive series of additions of feldspar. This eventually produced a melt but the colour was a particularly awful mud brown and the surface texture akin to the skin of a rice pudding! Having achieved, at least, a melt that was smooth and even, I chose to carry out another progressive series by adding whiting to the ash and feldspar mix. This time, at the fourth point in the series, there came a glaze of a dark grey, almost slate black colour that was matt in texture but turning black and glassy as it gathered in a fat roll at its margin. (See page 65.) It was a glaze not unlike some of the Northern Chinese tenmokus. At last, I had a glaze that seemed to say something about coal ash as a material in its own right. The eventual percentage recipe for this glaze was:

Coal ash	55
Whiting	19
Feldspar	26

As a second line of enquiry I decided to see what would happen if I tried to flux the coal ash (bearing in mind that the coal ash is more akin to an iron-bearing clay than a wood ash) with a fairly large percentage of whiting. (I could have chosen to do this with wood ash but I wanted to restrict the iron content to that in the coal ash.) The first test in this series was:

Coal ash	40 parts
Whiting	30 parts

which produced a dry surface that ran to any prominence. There was obviously a surfeit of calcia and a deficiency of silica. My next step was to add further additions of 15 parts of quartz to the base

above. (See page 65.) The results were a progressively shinier and more full-bodied glaze as the silica content became greater. Numbers 3 and 4 are both interesting glazes; Number 3, particularly, has a reserved quality and an unusual grey/green colour that I like. For practical purposes I added a small percentage of clay to the recipe which did not alter the fired quality of the glaze. The eventual percentage recipe for the final test in the series was:

Coal ash	31	
Whiting	23	
Quartz	34	
SMD ball clay	12	Fired to 1280°C

A bottle by the Author, 9" high.
This bottle has been brushed with a thick white slip immediately after turning. I try to create a pattern of movement with the brushstrokes and a feeling of the pot having been 'wrapped' up like the string around a parcel. This technique, known as hakame, came originally from Yi period Korea and grew out of a desire to prevent white slips from lifting away from the body of the pot as they were prone to do. It was found that if the slip were brushed on, it achieved a better adherence. The technique was later adopted by the Japanese as a decorative motif. I have drawn a toothed wooden tool through the wet slip quickly to produce a direct and sweeping mark with no hint of hesitation.

The pot was biscuit fired and then covered in the same straw ash glaze as the bowls in the colour plate on page 33.

A glaze containing a high percentage of coal ash that seems to say something to me about coal ash as a material and the sort of effects that I might expect to obtain from it.

Although the glaze has begun to run, the surface has remained crystalline, evidence perhaps of a surfeit of calcia. Here we have a starting point for further development.

These bowls show a progressive increase in quartz of 15 parts from left to right. Although it's a little difficult to see in the photograph, the first in the series, coal ash 40, whiting 30 is barely a glass at all. Even the high silica content of the coal ash cannot absorb such a massive amount of calcia. The glaze is dry and rough to the touch except where it has run but even here there the glass has devitrified. Overall it shows signs of far too great a calcia content. However, each time I added 15 parts of quartz to the base, the glaze became glassier and thicker. Numbers three and four are very nice, muted grey/green glazes, and in the case of Number four, similar to certain Korean celadons of the Koryo period.

The final recipe for Number three is:

Coal ash	35
Whiting	26
Quartz	26
SMD ball clay	13

And Number four:

Coal ash	31
Whiting	23
Quartz	34
SMD ball clay	12

The clay was added to aid slop suspension and to make the dry glazed pots a little less friable. There was no appreciable difference in the fired appearance.

I later ran the whole series again, this time substituting beech wood ash for the whiting and the fired results were very similar. There was little difference to the colour though I had suspected there might have been because of the iron content of the ash.

Applying the Ash Glaze

The range of ash glazes that I use tend to be those known as ash celadons and of all the glazes available to the potter, they are possibly the easiest to apply to the pot. I either dip or, when the pots are too large, pour my glazes. The ash, feldspar and clay mixtures always provide flat, even coatings. The occasional dribble can be ignored as this will disappear with the general movement of the glaze during firing. Other potters, some featured in this book, use a spray gun to apply their glaze. I have never used this type of equipment though the potential for control of glaze thickness is obvious. It is deceptively difficult to gauge though. *You should not consider this as a method unless you have an extracting spray booth or you can work out of doors*. Considering the expense of the equipment, the wastage of materials, the difficulties involved and the risks to health I would steer clear of spraying your glaze unless the effects you require in your work absolutely demand it.

The following is a guide to successful, consistent glazing. Bear in mind that, for me at least, most of the decorating has been done in the clay prior to the bisque fire. Glazing, by and large, is a straightforward covering over of this decoration. If, in your work, glazes are used one over another or you employ a wax resist technique or brushwork then you will have to modify these rules to suit your style of working. The great watchword is organisation and this applies however you work.

DO make sure that you have a container of clean water (warm in winter!) and two or three different sized sponges.

An eccentric teapot by Terry Bell-Hughes, 6" high.
The technique of dusting the dry glaze powder over the pot rather than dipping or pouring a liquid glaze slip was the earliest known method of deliberately applying a glazed surface to a pot. This teapot was first glazed with a rich, shiny tenmoku and then ash from a fine sieve has been sifted over selected areas to create a textured green 'patch'. The calcia in the ash has absorbed and bleached the iron oxide from the tenmoku to provide a mid-tone olive celadon.

DO check that you have sufficient glaze in the bin to allow for the glazing of your largest pot. If the largest pot is too big either for the bin or for you to hold then do as I do. Find a wide container (I use an old photographer's developing tray on the floor), perch the pot on two battens or wires over the tray having previously placed the tray on a heavy bench whirler. You can now pour your glaze over the, usually, upturned pot while it revolves on the bench whirler.

DO NOT use a new batch of an ash glaze that hasn't already been tested in the previous firing. A new batch may need some minor adjustment before it fires the way you want it to. I find this rule also applies to high-iron glazes as iron oxides can vary in strength from one batch or supplier to another.

DO make certain that your glazes are the correct thickness. Ash glazes need particular care over the correct thickness of application.

DO NOT glaze anything until you have thoroughly stirred the glaze. Never glaze more than three pots in a row without re-stirring.

DO keep a separate jug for each glaze.

A porcelain bottle by Derek Clarkson, 7¼" high.
When is an ash glaze not an ash glaze? To my mind any glaze that contains wood ash in whatever proportion is an 'ash' glaze. Often, as in the case of this porcelain bottle by Derek Clarkson, the ash in a glaze is there to modify the surface quality instead of completely taking over. The recipe for this glaze is:

Cornish stone	51
Ball clay	23
China clay	5
Whiting	3
Talc	5
Wood ash	13

1280°C. Heavy reduction from 960°C to the end of the firing.

This bottle is a fine example of a thoroughly professional approach to working. The glaze has been applied generously and evenly and to within a millimetre of the base. It is a stiff glaze that would show any runs or dribbles after firing and great care has been taken in the dipping to avoid any overlaps.

Do not expect the kind of superb finish that Derek has achieved here if you are not prepared to pay as much attention to detail as he does!

The glaze has a velvet, buttery feel and is particularly suitable for brush decoration. The two pigments that Derek has used are:

Blue	Cobalt carbonate	8
	Red iron oxide	3
	China clay	0.5
Rust	Red iron oxide	10
	China clay	0.5

MAKE SURE that you have a work surface free and uncluttered on which you can safely put down the freshly glazed pot. There's nothing that will raise the blood pressure quicker than running around the workshop like a headless chicken in the fruitless search for a space on which to put down a wet pot.

DO practise the trickery of glazing: Pouring out the glaze from the inside of a tall cylinder shape so as to glaze the whole of the inside evenly and the different ways of holding a pot for dipping because this can be difficult at first.

DO NOT try to save a badly glazed pot by touching it up with a paintbrush or even worse your fingers. The likelihood is that it will just get worse. Wash the glaze off, dry the pot and start again.

DO try to handle the glazed ware as little as possible. Use a board to carry the pots to the kiln and never pick up a glazed pot by its rim or handle.

1 This sequence of photographs show the glazing of a simple tea bowl. No matter how small or simple the shape all the rules in the text apply. Be organised!

Pour the glaze into the bowl up to the rim and leave for a couple of seconds.

2 Gently and without panic pour the glaze out of the bowl and back into the glaze bin.

LASTLY be organised. Don't allow your workspace to become cluttered, keep the surface in front of you free from unglazed pots and general debris. Panic will set in only when space is short or something that you need isn't to hand.

3 Now gently with an even pressure push the pot into the re-stirred glaze up to the point where you wish the glaze to stop, in this case as far as the foot.

4 Leave the pot submerged for a second or two (this sort of timing comes with experience and may differ from glaze to glaze) and then gently withdraw it. Once out of the glaze hold it for a few seconds to allow any drips to fall away and then slide it on to a clean surface with the fingertips.

5 The glazed bowl ready for the kiln.

The Use of Slips with Ash Glazes

In the workshop I keep three slips for use underneath the ash glazes. By using these slips I can achieve four different colours and surface textures from the same glaze covering. Applying a slip at the leather hard stage of the making process has obvious creative potential in itself although with any glaze that has a high calcia content one is limited in the effects that can be achieved with iron-bearing slips. *Note*: high calcia glazes will run and diffuse if placed over an iron slip thus destroying any pattern made in the underlying slip coat.

The photograph on p. 70 shows four bowls each glazed in the same straw ash glaze of:

Straw ash	56	
Potash feldspar	23	
China clay	3	
Whiting	8	
Talc	5	
Quartz	5	Fired to 1280°C

Bowl *Number 1* is the glaze alone, a medium celadon that sometimes shows a golden colour on edges and rims.

Number 2 is the same glaze over a white slip of:

Molochite	1 third
SMD ball clay	2 thirds

The glaze is now lighter in tone and tends towards yellow in places. It is overall less shiny and has an attractive crystalline structure in certain areas.

Number 3 has underneath a thin slip made from a sandy, iron-bearing clay that I find in the woods above the pottery. I call it an ochre but I am not sure that this is strictly accurate. The glaze has now fluxed a little more, due to the iron and possible further additions of flux in the slip. We have now a much deeper, dark honey-coloured glaze still with a crystalline surface in certain areas. It breaks very nicely in certain areas to a golden yellow colour.

Number 4 has a high iron slip of:

SMD ball clay	50 parts
China clay	50 parts
Red iron oxide	8 parts

We now have a rich, dark glaze that will run if not watched very carefully.

So you see, four different finishes but only one glaze. Of all these slips, I use the white most often.

My glazes, particularly those made with hardwoods, seem to improve when over this white slip. They often change their surface character to become something akin to the softest marble while the greens that appear as the glaze thickens become clear, clean and jewel-like.

In oxidation there is much less interaction between slip and glaze. The photograph on page 82 of a pot by Takeshi Yasuda shows an ash-type glaze over a white base slip. The glaze has stayed very much as a top coating while the slip acts as a mask to create a good white background for the flowing green and brown colouring. In an oxidised fire the iron in a high-iron slip will not behave as such a strong flux as it does in reducing conditions. Therefore, its colouring effect on the glaze will be less effective. There is scope here for some experimentation, perhaps the inclusion of some glaze fluxes within the slip which might render it more willing to mingle with the glaze during the firing.

A small dish, 6" diameter.
This small dish from Japan has been covered in a fairly thick white slip. The two leaf shapes are the result of pressing the leaves into the surface of the clay prior to applying the slip and then removing them after the slip has dried a little. The ash glaze has formed itself into a mottled texture akin to salt glaze and is pale yellow in colour.

This technique is so simple that it could easily be overdone, although as in this case, when handled with restraint and understatement, the effect is to create a feeling of leaves floating to earth on a quiet autumn evening.
Collection of Gas Kimishima.

Firing the Glaze

Ash glazes in an oxidised fire

I think that it is fairly true to say that ash-based glazes require a reduction firing to bring out their best qualities, but then, I am biased. One only has to look at the photograph on page 82 of the pot of Takeshi Yasuda to realise that the electric kiln need never be an obstacle to beautiful work.

This tiny model of a blanket chest required a matt glaze that would highlight the structure and enhance the detail in the small pots. The colour is an Indian red with a lighter ochre mottled surface where the glaze has been applied thicker:

Wood ash	50	
Red earthenware clay	50	Oxidised firing 1280°.

You will have to experiment with various red clays to achieve the desired effect. I used Etruria Marl in this instance although it was some twenty years ago!

Some years ago I used only an electric kiln and developed a number of ash glazes that were suitable for domestic stoneware along with some that were more suitable for sculptural ceramics. My approach in finding these glazes was exactly as outlined earlier, line and tri-axial blends of ash with various materials such as clays, dolomite or nephaline syenite. I have included some of these recipes for oxidation at the back of the book.

Katherine Pleydell-Bouverie first used an electric kiln in 1960 and achieved wonderful results, often at quite low temperatures, by the addition of small quantities of low temperature frits and colouring oxides.

With the advent of materials such as ceramic fibre and new firebricks with exceptional insulating properties, plus a new understanding of kiln design,

there is no reason why anyone should have an electric kiln unless they especially want one. Gone are the days when a gas kiln meant a long, conspicuous chimney or the need to have a floor strengthened. I have a small kiln here at the pottery that can easily be lifted by two people and is transportable in the back of the car. It requires no chimney, the flue is an integral part of the chamber, and it is incredibly cheap to fire.

For those able and interested in building a small kiln that can be be fired with propane or natural gas, I can do no better than direct you to the late Andrew Holden's book, *The Self Reliant Potter*, in which you will find the plans and instructions to build a small kiln of this type.

Reduction firing

Essentially, all the factors that govern stoneware temperature glaze firing apply to the ash glaze. Careful attention should be given to the kiln throughout the firing to ensure that it has proceeded in the same way as the last successful firing. A carefully annotated logbook will help you in this. I fire all of my pots in a reduction atmosphere and I have noticed one or two important points during the firing of ash glazes that are worthy of special mention.

Firstly, as I have already mentioned, high ash content glazes tend to begin their melting process quite early in the firing, around 1050°C. I find that it is important to proceed to the temperature where reduction starts quite slowly. This will help overcome any tendency for blistering that may occur (this is discussed on p. 72) and ensure that the body is well reduced under the glaze coating. As soon as any fusion of the glaze layer takes place this effectively seals off the clay body underneath and any further reduction to the body becomes impossible. The result is a nasty whiteness showing through on edges rather than the rich tan that I normally expect.

Secondly, I find the cooling of the kiln very important in achieving that special mix of matt, crystalline areas with shinier, glassy parts. It is always the case that a fast cooling kiln will inhibit the growth of crystals in a glaze. I have found that my glazes behave very differently in one of the new fast-firing, fast-cooling ceramic fibre kilns — without exception they are cleaner, shinier and display less typical ash qualities. If you use one of these kilns you may need to take steps to try and retard the cooling cycle. In my large, oil-fired brick kiln I cool

Colour test 7

quickly to around 1100°C and then close off all the secondary air ports to facilitate as slow a cool as possible to the point at which I can break the wicket and unpack. You may find that this practice may not suit all your other glazes. Tenmokus, for instance, tend to prefer a faster cool and may need a separate fire.

Below is a typical firing graph for my 75 cu. ft. oil-fired kiln.

7 This plate shows the effects that different slips can have on the same top glaze. Each bowl has been glazed with the same straw ash glaze with, from right to left.

1 Glaze alone
2 White slip underneath
3 Local ochre slip underneath
4 High iron slip

Not only are the colours different but the surface quality varies also.

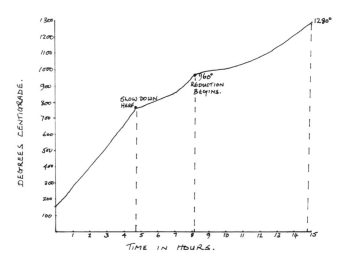

Ash glazes in the salt kiln

Firing a 'salt kiln' is much like firing a normal stoneware reduction kiln. The big difference is that the pots can be placed in the kiln without any covering of conventional glaze. When the kiln is approaching the white heat of 1260°C, almost at the point that an ordinary firing would be over, common salt (NaCl) is thrown into the fireboxes in the direct path of the flame from the burners. On meeting the intense heat of the furnace the salt immediately volatilises to form sodium vapour. This gaseous soda then reacts with the silica in the pottery body to form a glaze. In my own kiln this

process of salting may take as long as two hours before a sufficient thickness of glaze has accumulated on the surface of the pots.

When I began to make salt-glazed pots it was perhaps only to be expected that I would place an ash-glazed pot into a salt firing to 'see what would happen'. In fact I had a pretty good idea that the experiment would be a success. Some 50 years ago, Denise Wren had carried out some work with salted ash glazes and then much later, a British potter, Walter Keeler (amongst others), found that the ash celadon-type glaze was perfectly suitable for use in the salt kiln.

The effect of the salt is to provide an extra flux to the glaze. The result is a glaze surface that often begins to flow down the pot gathering itself into rivulets as it does. See the photograph on page 71. The effect can be highly decorative. The salt also has a bleaching effect on the iron. Most glazes will emerge from the salt kiln much lighter in tone than they normally fire. The two bowls in the colour photograph on page 71 show this effect. Both bowls have the same glaze. The one on the left has been salted and, quite plainly, is a lighter colour to the one on the right.

In the case of the two bowls in the colourplate the glaze is the straw ash mentioned earlier (p. 68). However, I normally use an adapted version of my standard pine ash glaze. This glaze contains a little more China clay to counteract a tendency to run and a little more iron to retain a decisive colour.

The two bowls in this plate have both been glazed with my straw ash glaze but then the left-hand bowl was placed in a salt glaze firing while the other had a normal reduction firing.

The bowl on the left is much paler in colour, the result of the bleaching action of the salt upon the iron in the glaze.

A faceted bottle by the Author, 12" high.
This bottle has been glazed with an ash glaze of:

Ash	56	
Potash feldspar	24.5	
China clay	14	
Whiting	4	
Red iron oxide	2	1280°C

The extra fluxing power of the soda from the salt has increased the fluidity of the ash glaze. The small amount of iron added to the glaze is to counteract the tendency of the salt to bleach away the colour.

Glaze Faults

In working with high ash content glazes one is not so prone to the glaze faults that can occur with other glazes and I would refer the reader to a book that deals with the common glaze faults in some detail as it isn't really applicable here. Having decided to work with ash glazes it is more often than not the case that there is an acceptance of what other potters may regard as glaze 'faults' as part of the inherent character and charm of this type of glaze.

Crazing, for instance, is part and parcel of an ash glaze and accounts for much of the character of an

A large jar by American potter Karen Karnes, 25 cm.
This imposing jar has been saltglazed having first had an application of an ash celadon. The extra fluidity of the ash glaze is due to the extra flux in the form of soda supplied by the salt.

A glaze that behaves very much as the one in the photograph is:

Ash	70
Feldspar	30
China clay	20
Quartz	25
Red iron oxide	2

Courtesy of Christies Ltd.

ash celadon. Additions of quartz or flint will probably reduce the crazing but in doing so will also rob it of its inherent charm. Crazing (see Glossary) is almost inevitable in a glaze that has a deficiency in silica and relies on potash and soda and to a lesser extent calcia and its fluxes. For this reason the fault known as **Shivering** (see Glossary), the flaking away of areas of glaze especially on rims or handles, which technically speaking is the opposite of crazing, hardly ever occurs in a high ash content glaze.

Crawling, which is the tendency for a glaze to lift itself from the surface of the pot and gather in beads or droplets, is also rare and seldom happens because of the ash glaze itself. It is more likely that the pot was dusty or greasy prior to glazing and this prevented the proper adherence of the glaze slip during glazing.

In general terms, the high content ash glaze is an extremely tolerant 'partner'. There are really only two faults that can be attributed to the glaze rather than the person carrying out the glazing and these are relatively easily overcome.

Running of the glaze due to insufficient alumina can be a nuisance. With ash glazes we rely on some movement of the glaze for its character and we often walk a tightrope between a glaze that is too static and one that is too runny. An addition of clay will cure this, often without any loss of surface quality; a progression blend will ascertain how much to add. However, I believe that it is better to lose the occasional pot in the interest of achieving the quality you require on all the other pots. I fire most of my pots on alumina/China clay wads which lift the pot off the kiln shelf enough so that if running does occur then usually the pot isn't ruined. A few moments' use of the bench grinder and a silicon carbide pad is all that is required.

A fault that I have experienced that proved not so easy to cure was **blistering**. For a period, a few years ago, I became plagued with small, sharp blisters on the outside of my pots. I tried a number of different ploys to try and cure the problem all to no avail. These included a change of feldspar, sieving my ash through a finer mesh, a change of body recipe and a new fireclay. The new fireclay improved things but didn't completely cure the problem.

I began to think in terms of the firing as a possible cause. At first I took extra special care with the bisque fire. I made sure it was long and clean with at least $2\frac{1}{2}$ hours during the critical period of 850°C to 1000°C, the point when any residual carbonaceous matter is burnt out. No effect!

My next move was to lengthen the glaze fire up to 1000°C, the point that I began reduction. The previous $4\frac{1}{2}$ hours became 8 hours and behold! the problem was solved. In my ignorance I hadn't realised that the high ash content glaze, because of the readiness of its alkaline fluxes to melt, begins to melt early in a stoneware firing. This early fusing seals off the pot's surface thereby locking in any unwanted gaseous material. I believe that I had unwittingly been sealing in sulphur, the product of sulphates that existed in the clay *and the wood ash*, that then bubbled its way upward through my glaze leaving the blister as its calling card. Be aware that high content ash glazes do not like to be fired too quickly especially between 850°C and 1050°C.

Glaze thickness

All glazes are subject to changes in their appearance due to inconsistencies in the thickness of the glaze coat. None more so than ash glazes. Whilst this susceptibility may provide scope for creative glazing, pouring, double dipping, etc., I include it here as a fault, not in the glaze but with the glazer. Too often I have seen a good pot spoilt either because the glaze slop was too thin and therefore deposited an insufficient coating all over the pot or, alternatively, the glaze hadn't been properly stirred since glazing the previous pot. This error tends to produce an uneven coating which can range from perfect thickness to a thin, brown, varnish-like covering. Get to know the optimum thicknesses for your glazes. If you find this difficult, then weigh a pint of the glaze and make sure that before you next use it, the 'pint weight' as we call it, is the same. Around 30 ounces to the pint would be a reasonable weight to begin with although, I have to say, I have never found it necessary to find a pint weight. You will very quickly come to recognise the correct thickness just by its appearance in the glaze bin.

Points to Remember

As you will have no doubt already concluded there is little that is scientific in this sort of approach to glaze making. All that is required is an inquisitive nature and enough of a working knowledge of the potter's raw materials to be able to make an educated guess.

YOU MUST, however, keep detailed records of your experiments; never trust anything to memory. Make sure that your test pieces are clearly marked with the test series and number, and enter a brief description of the results in a notebook. Having found a glaze that you really like and wish to use in some quantity, move its recipe to a different notebook, or as I now do to a computer disc, and keep it safe. Don't do as I once did, take the glaze book away from the studio and lose it.

I always need to test my glazes under the effects of gravity so I never use tiles. Rather I use small bowls which I throw quickly 'off the hump'. This way I can tell exactly the amount of movement in a glaze and prevent disaster later with a larger piece.

NEVER throw away test pieces however bad you may think they are at the time. It is amazing how your tastes and expectations will change. I often sort through old glaze tests and find one that I discarded at the time which, after the passage of years, is now exactly what I am looking for. At the very least, old test pieces can often provide clues as to where to proceed with a current series or encourage you to examine again the effects of the inclusion of certain materials.

ALWAYS, when dealing with wood ashes or local materials, make sure that their containers are clearly marked with either the type of ash or the source of the stone and the date you acquired them. Ashes and stone dusts all look remarkably similar and major, costly mistakes can happen if you mix a glaze with one material believing it to be another.

ALWAYS test a glaze sample in different parts of the kiln. I always dip at least three of any particular mix. Make sure that if you suspect a test may be a 'runner' that you fire it on a small, scrap piece of kiln shelf or alumina wads. This will protect your expensive kiln bats. After a very short time you will begin to understand the results of your endeavours as they come from the kiln. Don't be afraid of making mistakes; often, interesting glazes can come from the most unlikely combinations of materials.

DON'T forget that you can try blending glazes together. Sometimes two glazes that are less than exciting can produce something far better when put together. Try line blending your glazes or adding one to another in a progressive series. Keep your eyes open for interesting effects when one glaze is over another. I have found that this occurrence has led to new glazes when the two in question are blended and applied to the pot as one.

REMEMBER: all glazes require silica (the glass former), all glazes require fluxes to melt the silica and all glazes require alumina as a bonding agent or stabiliser. If you remember this general guideline then you will have understood the very basic principle of glaze making.

In general terms, when dealing with wood ash one has accounted for the fluxes so we need only to find the correct additions of silica and alumina to achieve the effect required. When we have an unknown stone or clay then, we must think in terms of additions of the right amount of fluxes and perhaps extra silica to provide a melt. When I have a new stone to work with, for the initial tests at least, I simply regard it as feldspar and see what happens.

Constant testing for new glazes can be exciting and rewarding work. It can also become obsessive to the detriment of one's own potting. There is little point to a workshop packed with more glazes than one person can possibly use. Much better to find a few that can become good and reliable friends whilst always being on the lookout to extend one's range within the parameters you have already set yourself.

REMEMBER, before a glaze is worth anything you must have a good pot to put it on. The very best of glazes never rescued a bad form. I have noticed that it is often the case that those people who make it their life's work to know everything about the chemistry of glazes and test and test ad infinitum are seldom the best potters. I am not sure that this is because the glaze work is compensation for poor pots or because the work with the glazes has left so little time for potting!

In Conclusion

If we decide to apply ourselves to any form of craft we have a duty to try and make whatever it is we are involved with to the very best of our ability. The world is a cluttered enough place without the thumb fingered and careless work that so often haunts what has euphemistically come to be known as the 'Craft' shop.

As far as we potters are concerned there is so much that is of excellent quality to be seen that there is no excuse for not being familiar with fine quality ceramics. Look around, get to know where the galleries and shops in your area are. Visit them, handle the pots, appreciate their qualities, decide what it is that makes a pot 'good' for you and try to introduce these qualities into your own work. Search out the public collections of studio pottery. I am lucky — I live very near to one of the best collections in the UK at Aberystwyth, and even luckier, some of my pots are in it!

I hope that this book will have helped you to understand some of the problems and delights of working with glazes and in particular the use of wood and vegetable ashes which make up just a small fraction of the total possibilities of clay and glaze. If I have motivated you to find some ash and begin some experiments then I have succeeded in what I set out to do. It was never my intention to baffle and confuse with unnecessary scientific detail,

I merely wanted to show that an appreciation of the minerals and materials immediately around us can bring forth pots of a truly individual character together with immeasurable satisfaction.

A bottle 12" high by Mike Dodd.
Seek out exemplary pots, pick them up, feel them, their surface and their weight. Look at the form, try to decide why it looks so 'right'. Examine the relationships of height to width or diameter of base to width of neck. Ask yourself, where is the widest point? and then why is it there and not higher or lower?

Draw it. There is no better way, however good or bad your drawing, to imprint a detail upon the memory. Only by asking yourself or discussing these questions with others can you begin to develop an intuitive feel for rightness and quality.

Ash-like Glazes without Ash

I am firmly of the belief that wood ash imparts certain qualities to a glaze that cannot be reproduced by any other means. I must say it came as something of a surprise when recently that belief was tested to the limit.

A young man, who had been a student in our summer school, came to visit some months later in order to show me some pots that he had made since being with us. He had taken away with him my ash glaze recipes but had found it difficult to find a reasonable quantity of ash to work with. Instead, he found the late Andrew Holden's book, *The Self-Reliant Potter*, from which he took the recipe for a wood ash substitute and reconstructed the glaze batch using Holden's recipe. The results were very impressive.

The glazes looked very much like my own originals although I did feel that there was missing a certain, almost indescribable quality. They lacked the depth I normally look for and were of a single surface texture, a little too shiny. But they were very good, very good indeed! And who is to say that with a little judicious alteration they couldn't have been made even better?!

To a purist like myself, the idea of producing a 'synthetic' ash may seem a little strange. After all, it is the very unpredictable nature of the material that is part of its attraction. However, for the potter who has difficulty in obtaining wood ash or if a supply has come to an end or unpredictability is not a desired feature, then an ash substitute may be a realistic alternative. It also means, that on a theoretical level at least, any plant or wood ash is available to us providing that we have both the analysis and the means of turning that analysis into a batch recipe. We should remember though, that the manner in which the different oxides are combined in a natural ash makes it difficult to recreate exactly all the subtle characteristics we look for in an ash glaze.

We have already seen that wood ash is composed of the same oxides that make up the minerals from which the plant drew its nutrition during growth. It is then, once we have an analysis, a relatively simple matter to translate the oxide or elemental analysis of the ash into a batch recipe that uses the raw materials commonly used in glaze making. Don't forget what we said earlier, the raw materials, as supplied to you, are, with very few exceptions, mixtures of oxides. The problem that we have to overcome is how to sort out, from the choice of materials available to us, the right minerals and in what quantities so as to provide a more or less exact replica, in oxide terms, of our wood ash sample.

It's worth remembering here that the variability of composition between woods of the same species actually assists us in this. We don't need to worry about being super accurate in our reconstruction as any minor discrepancy many only represent the variance, probably in smaller terms, from one actual sample to another.

In my own work with ash glazes I rarely use mathematics. This is for two reasons. First, and quite simply, I have never really had the need to reconstruct an ash. I have always managed to manufacture or scrounge all the wood ash that I ever wanted and mathematics has little or no place in the construction of my wood ash glaze recipes.

Secondly and equally simple is the fact that I am a mathematical dunce. If there is a mathematical equivalent for dyslexia, then I have it! Figures have always

This bowl shows two of my ash glazes reconstructed using widely available potters raw materials as an ash substitute. In these two instances the results were very impressive although they lack a little of the glaze body interaction that I normally look for in an ash glaze. This is due to the complete lack of any soluble fluxes which would normally be taken into the body layer on dipping. One could introduce some soluble alkaline material in the form of potassium carbonate or soda ash or even a small amount of common salt which would improve matters.

The ash was replaced by the following formula:

Potash feldspar	10
Whiting	60
Talc	5
Bone ash	5
Ball clay	15
Quartz	5

which represents a 'washed' mixed ash.

The eventual recipes for the complete glazes are as follows:

Pale green 'ash' celadon	1280°C
Potash feldspar	19
Whiting	31
Talc	2.4
Bone ash	2.4
Ball clay	6
Quartz	9
Cornish stone	15
China clay	15

White 'Nuka'	1280°C
Potash feldspar	36
Whiting	22
Talc	2
Bone ash	2
Ball clay	6
Quartz	30
Boro-calcite frit	3

been a struggle for me and that is possibly one of the reasons that led me along the wood ash path in the first place. Being essentially a self-taught potter I shied away from what seemed to me, in the early days at least, to be rather complicated mathematics. So, let it be a comfort to the wary reader, that if I can perform the following calculations (with the help of a calculator!) then anybody can.

To enable us to overcome, what at first glance seems, an almost insurmountable problem we can use a slightly adapted version of the Seger formula. Remember, in the following calculations we are **not** creating glazes but passable alternatives for individual ashes that can then be included as part of a glaze recipe batch.

Hermann Seger and his Formula

During the 19th century, a German chemist, Hermann Seger (1839–94), applied himself to overcoming certain problems within ceramics. One of these was the difficulty of comparing glaze formulae with one to another; in particular the difficulties of seeing quickly the ratio of silica to the fluxes in a glaze and how that ratio compared to that of another glaze. He conceived a method of expressing a glaze by the proportions of the constituent molecules. He did this by grouping all the different oxides within the glaze into three separate categories: the fluxes, the stabiliser and the acidic glass formers. The chemist refers to this trio as the RO/R_2O, R_2O_3, and the RO_2 groups when R is taken to mean the root or radical and is substituted for each of the chemical symbols in each element that is combined with oxygen. Dividing each figure in an oxide percentage analysis by the molecular weight of each oxide results in a list which represents the ratios of molecules in that analysis.

If the total of all the fluxes in the glaze add up to one, it becomes much easier to establish the silica to flux ratio in a single glaze or to compare one glaze with another.

This calculation has come to be known as the Seger or Unity formula and for a detailed description and information on the full potential of this system I would refer the reader to Daniel Rhodes's book *Clay and Glazes for the Potter*. It is a system that, for the non-chemist, is not easy to understand. We are all used to dealing with weights of substances, but with Seger we have to get used to dealing with the comparative numbers of molecules, an entirely different and somewhat abstract concept. Rhodes remains unsurpassed in his ability to explain a complicated theory in relatively simple, easily understood terms.

For our purposes, we really do not have to worry about the intricacies of glaze calculation if we don't want to. I have devised a straightforward series of calculations, based on the Seger formula, that will convert the analysis of any wood or plant ash or local rock into a batch formula. It's not even necessary to understand the theory behind the calculation if you don't want to. However, if you progress through the following steps, merely substituting your analysis for mine you will arrive at a reasonable batch formula. If you do this having read Chapter 12 in *Clay and Glazes for the Potter* then so much the better.

Let's take for our example an analysis for ashwood ash documented by Katherine Pleydell-Bouverie. We have to assume, until we have the opportunity to test our effort, that the analysis is fairly reliable. It is as follows:

Silica (SiO$_2$)	23.30	Calcia (CaO)	25.52
Potash (K$_2$O)	16.02	Soda (Na$_2$O)	7.65
Magnesia (MgO)	12.00	Phosphorus pentoxide (P$_2$O$_5$)	57.00
Alumina (Al$_2$O$_3$)	0.63	Ferric oxide (iron) (Fe$_2$O$_3$)	3.92
Manganous oxide (MnO)	0.41		

(For the purpose of this reconstruction I have ignored the small percentage of sulphate which contributes little or nothing to the glaze and might even be injurious in that a sulphate presence could induce blistering and/or frothing. I have experienced both in the past. However, while the blistering was due to sulphates within the body and therefore not a glaze fault as such, the frothing, where the glaze has run a little thick, is so rare as not to be worth worrying about. I have also left out the chloride fraction. If it's found desirable to include a soluble chloride, then a small quantity of common salt can be added to the glaze batch. Tichane tells us that although the quantity of chloride in wood ash is probably never more than 1%, it does have a marked influence on glazes in that, due to its volatile nature, it encourages the migration of iron, both in the body and in the glaze. It is noticeable that when a pot is glazed in a high

ash content glaze, especially in oxidation where the body stays light in colour, a brown to orange stain appears just below the glaze line. This is due, in part, to soluble alkalis having been taken up by the body and then diffusing to give a thin varnish-like effect outside the glazed area. Any chloride present will increase this effect particularly in relation to the amount of iron carried to the surface. If you think back to the comments I made about the glazes made by my student, it is possible that their lack of quality was due to a reduced amount of glaze/body interaction because Holden did not include any soluble material in his ash substitute formula.)

Step one

We take the analysis above and express it as a glaze formula according to the Seger principle. Remember that although we are dealing only with a single ash analysis, most ashes will melt to a glass when fired alone and therefore in this context can be regarded as a glaze 'recipe'. For this we need a worksheet as follows:

OXIDE	AW.	MW.	MP.
SILICA SiO$_2$.			
POTASH K$_2$O.	16.02	94.2	0.170
MAGNESIA MgO.			
ALUMINA. Al$_2$O$_3$.			
CALCIA. CaO			
SODA. Na$_2$O			
PHOSPHORUS PENTOXIDE P$_2$O$_5$			
IRON FeO			
MANGANOUS OXIDE. MnO			

All the constituent parts of Pleydell-Bouverie's analysis are listed down the left-hand side of the sheet under the heading, Oxide. In the next column we have the percentages of these oxides present (Actual Weight, AW). We now have to find the proportion of the molecules of each ingredient in the analysis. To do this we must divide each quantity by its own molecular weight. A list of the molecular weights for the oxides commonly found in ashes can be found at the back of the book. Thus, we can enter the molecular weights in the next column (MW).

For example:

$$\frac{\text{Potash, Actual parts by weight}}{\text{Molecular weight}} = \text{Mol. parts}$$

$$\frac{\text{Potash, 16.02}}{\text{M.W. 94.2}} = 0.1700636$$

For our purposes three decimal places are sufficient so we have:

0.170. Molecular parts.

The molecular parts can now be entered into the fourth column (MP).

We now continue (with the calculator) in the same manner until the sheet looks like this:

OXIDE	AW.	MW.	MP.
SILICA SiO_2	23.30	60.1	0.387
POTASH K_2O	16.02	94.2	0.170
MAGNESIA MgO	12.00	40.3	0.297
ALUMINA Al_2O_3	0.63	102	0.006
CALCIA CaO	25.52	56.1	0.454
SODA Na_2O	7.65	62	0.123
PHOSPHORUS PENTOXIDE P_2O_5	7	142	0.049
IRON FeO	3.92	78.1	0.050
MANGANOUS OXIDE. MnO	.41	86.9	0.004

As I mentioned before, this is a slightly simplified conversion because the wood ash ingredients are all single oxides. One can imagine that if we wanted to express a glaze recipe as a Seger Formula we would be dealing with raw materials that contain a number of different oxides within themselves. Potash feldspar for example, contains the oxides of potassium, aluminium and silicon and each would have to be entered onto the grid with due regard to the number of molecules of each oxide present. Again, this further complication is dealt with in Rhodes's book and in the interests of simplicity does not concern us in this context.

Potash	(K_2O)	.170				
Soda	(Na_2O)	.123				
Calcia	(CaO)	.454	Alumina (Al_2O_3)	.006	Silica	(SiO_2)	.387
Magnesia	(MgO)	.297			Phosphorus		
Iron	(FeO)	.050			pentoxide	(P_2O_5)	.049

What we have done in the above calculation is to express the physical weight of the ash constituents in terms of the chemical proportions present. The formula can be now written as shown at the bottom of the page.

In a complete Seger or Unity formula we would now make the total of all the oxides in the first column i.e. the fluxes, add up to one. To do this, find the total of all molecular parts in the flux column, in this case 1.094 and then divide each individual oxide by this total. Then divide all the other oxides in the formula by the same figure i.e. 1.094. This brings the formula to unity and the silica content in comparison to the fluxes can now be easily seen. The formula can now be written:

K_2O	.155				
Na_2O	.112				
CaO	.415			MnO	.003
MgO	.271	Al_2O_3	.005	SiO_2	.353
FeO	.045			P_2O_5	.044

.998

For our purposes this part of the calculation is not strictly necessary as we are only concerned with the molecular proportions within our ash analysis and not with any comparisons of one analysis with another.

Step two

We now have to take our formula and by studying it, decide in which raw materials we will find the oxides that are required to make up the ash equivalent. We obviously need potash and soda. These could come from using both potash and soda feldspar but unfortunately this analysis contains very little alumina and so the amount of feldspar we can use is severely limited. Perhaps we can use a little feldspar, just enough to supply the alumina required, and then make up the rest of the potash and soda with potassium carbonate and soda ash. These are both soluble however and may cause problems later on, although on the plus side their solubility will serve to reproduce certain characteristics of wood ashes previously discussed. Tichane tells us that a *Small* amount of potash feldspar could be used in place of all or some of the potassium carbonate if solubility is a problem or if one is concerned to reproduce a washed rather than an unwashed ash. He obviously isn't overly worried at the inclusion of a small amount of alumina in the batch.

The calcium can come from whiting but we also need to include some bone ash which also contains calcia so allowance has to be made for that. The silica can come partly from any feldspar we may use and the rest from flint or quartz. The iron is straightforward although in some recipes where clay can be used to supply alumina, it is better to use a ball clay with an iron content rather than neat iron oxide. This more successfully approximates the intimate way in which the iron is combined in an ash. This may complicate matters a little as ball clays do contain small quantities of some of the fluxes and this may need to be taken into account when making the batch. Dolomite can be our source of magnesium.

To sort out this mass of information requires another worksheet.

RAW MATERIAL	RATIO REQUIRED	K_2O .155	Na_2O .112	CaO .415	MgO .271	Al_2O_3 .005	SiO_2 .353	FeO .045	MnO .003	P_2O_5 .044
POTASSIUM CARBONATE K_2CO_3										
SODA FELDSPAR $Na_2O\ Al_2O_3\ 6SiO_2$										
SODA ASH Na_2CO_3										
BONE ASH $Ca_3(PO_4)_2$										
DOLOMITE $CaCO_3$										
WHITING $CaCO_3$										
QUARTZ SiO_2										
FERRIC OXIDE Fe_2O_3										
MANGANESE DIOXIDE MnO_2										

Down the left-hand side we list the minerals that we think will provide us with the required oxides. Include the chemical symbol for each mineral. Along the top of the sheet place the different oxides in their conventional order and underneath each one the quantity of that oxide required in the batch.

We can now fill in the chart, one material at a time as follows:

First, potassium carbonate. 0.155 of potassium is called for in the formula and as potassium carbonate contributes only potassium to the final ash substitute we can find all the potassium we need from this material. We can now write .155 in the K_2O column and in the ratio required column and then double underline the K_2O column to indicate that we have satisfied the potassium requirements.

The next material is soda feldspar which is a little more complex in that it contains three different oxides in differing amounts. Each molecule of feldspar contains one molecule of alumina (Al_2O_3), therefore the ratio of feldspar required is 1 times .005 = .005. This figure can be entered into the Al_2O_3 column. As feldspar contains one molecule of soda the same amount, .005 can be entered into the Na_2O column and then a single line is drawn underneath. The .005 figure is then subtracted from the total soda requirement and the difference is written below. Feldspar also contains six silica molecules. This means that for every given amount of either soda or alumina, feldspar will contribute six times that amount of silica. To take account of this amount of silica we must multiply .005 by 6 and enter this into the silica column and subtract from the total silica requirement.

RAW MATERIAL	RATIO REQUIRED	K_2O .155	Na_2O .112	CaO .415	MgO .271	Al_2O_3 .005	SiO_2 .353	FeO .045	MnO .003	P_2O_5 .044
POTASSIUM CARBONATE K_2CO_3	.155	.155								
SODA FELDSPAR $Na_2O\ Al_2O_3\ 6SiO_2$	.005		.005			.03				
SODA ASH Na_2CO_3			.107			.323				
BONE ASH $Ca_3(PO_4)_2$										
DOLOMITE $CaMg(CO_3)_2$										
WHITING $CaCO_3$										
QUARTZ SiO_2										
FERRIC OXIDE Fe_2O_3										
MANGANESE DIOXIDE MnO_2										

The rest of the chart is filled in using the same rules and should eventually look like this:

RAW MATERIAL	RATIO REQUIRED	K_2O .155	Na_2O .112	CaO .415	MgO .271	Al_2O_3 .005	SiO_2 .353	FeO .045	MnO .003	P_2O_5 .044
POTASSIUM CARBONATE K_2CO_3	.155	.155								
SODA FELDSPAR $Na_2O\ Al_2O_3\ 6SiO_2$	.005		.005			.005	.03			
SODA ASH Na_2CO_3	.107		.107				.323			
BONE ASH $Ca_3(PO_4)_2$	.044			.044						.044
DOLOMITE $CaMg(CO_3)_2$	.271			.371						
WHITING $CaCO_3$	.100			.271	.271					
QUARTZ SiO_2	.323				.100					
FERRIC OXIDE Fe_2O_3	.045							.045		
MANGANESE DIOXIDE MnO_2	.003								.003	

We have now discovered the ratio of the molecules of the raw materials required.

Step three

To find the physical weight of each material we have to multiply the ratio of each material by its own molecular weight:

	ratio	MW		Physical Weight
Potassium carbonate	.155	138.2	=	21.420
Soda feldspar	.005	524.6	=	2.620
Soda ash	.107	106	=	11.342
Bone ash	.044	310.3	=	13.653
Dolomite	.271	184.4	=	49.972
Whiting	.012	100	=	1.200
Quartz	.323	60.1	=	19.420
Iron	.045	71.8	=	3.230
Manganous oxide	.003	70.9	=	0.212

This recipe can now be converted to a percentage batch by dividing each individual amount by the sum total of all the amounts i.e. 123.069 and then multiplying by 100 thus:

		Rounded number
Potassium carbonate	17.40	17.00
Soda feldspar	2.12	2.25
Soda ash	9.21	9.25
Bone ash	11.09	11.00
Dolomite	40.60	40.50
Whiting	.90	1.00
Quartz	15.77	15.50
Iron	2.62	2.50
Manganous oxide	.17	.25

The second column is merely a version with the figures rounded up. This recipe is a theoretical representation of the original **unwashed** ash and therefore contains a higher proportion of soluble material. If your require a **washed** version, then a portion of the potassium carbonate, perhaps 50%, could be replaced with potash feldspar and the same substitution with soda feldspar for soda ash with the resulting addition of alumina ignored.

Please don't be put off by the thought of all these figures. It really isn't as complicated as it appears at first sight. Follow the calculation through step by step in a logical, organised fashion and you will be surprised how easy it really is. As I said before, I would strongly recommend the reading of Rhodes on the subject.

When I began this book I did not intend to include a chapter of this nature at all. However as

time went by my research led me to the conclusion that a discussion about ash substitutes would be appropriate and useful to many people for whom the gathering or processing of wood ash could be a problem; disabled potters, for instance could find this an easier approach.

Whilst I can see the interest value of an exercise like the one above, I would still prefer to use the real thing and accept its imperfections as an endearing quality. Where I can see a real use for calculations of this sort is to duplicate those ashes or local stones that geographically are difficult for me to obtain. I would hate to think that because of this book, potters used ash substitutes as a matter of course. Unlike Robert Tichane whose book is full of useful information but who seems to have completely missed the point of using ashes, I really believe that a substitute is just that and regardless of how good it can be should never replace the real thing without good reason.

Analysis and theory are useful tools in their right place but they should not be allowed to reign supreme. The dry, stifled world of figures will be reflected in boring, lifeless glazes. Mike Dodd, a British potter working in the north of England,

These two bowls allow us to compare a true ash and a reconstructed ash. The bowl on the right has a covering of pure beech ash and on the left I have taken the reconstructed formula for beech ash from below. You can see that apart from a minor difference in the tone of green there is very little difference at all! Each shows signs of having corroded the surface of the clay underneath, each has bleached the clay body and each has run off the pot!

On the basis of this trial I then mixed my standard ash glaze using both beech ash and the reconstructed beech ash. The results can be seen in colour test 9 on p. 82.

Again there was very little difference. The bowl on the left has the 'fake' ash and is showing signs of too much soluble content. The body below the glaze has begun to flux and has become very red in colour. This fault is easy to cure merely by leaving out much of the potassium carbonate and soda ash and replacing them with potash and soda feldspar.

produces some of the most beautiful, rich and exciting glazes that I have seen and he does this by the empirical use of local rocks and clays. He blends a logical, annotated series of experiments with an instinct based on experience to achieve wonderful results (See pp. 100–107.)

It is interesting to read Hamada on the subject of ashes and local materials in general. In his book on Hamada, Bernard Leach records him as saying,

How the two kinds of rice ash maintain their characteristics to the end, even when they are reduced to ash and fired to the temperature of 1300°C is really amazing – something out of nature that cannot be understood. Maybe we should leave the mystery as a mystery; it is no use trying to analyse it and understand it; rather than waste time on that, make something beautiful.

Hamada really understood the romance in the material.

Some recipes for ash substitutes

To get back to the subject of the chapter, I have carried out the same calculation for a number of different ash analyses and some of those results are as follows together with a number of different ash substitutes from other sources. These may provide an interesting jumping off point for further investigation.

1. Bernard Leach's analysis for rice straw ash can be reconstructed as follows:

China clay	20
Dolomite	3.5
Talc	13
Quartz	56.75
Potassium carbonate	2
Bone ash	2
FeO (iron)	2

The same ash can be interpreted as follows, this time using the insoluble form of potash as potash feldspar:

Potash feldspar	9
Dolomite	3.5
Bone ash	2
Talc	13.5
China clay	17.25
Quartz	55
FeO (iron)	1.5

2. The following are both for beech. The first, from an analysis of trunk wood and the second from branch wood.

(i)		
	Soda feldspar	22.75
	Dolomite	24.25
	Bone ash	6
	Whiting	34
	Soda ash	4
	Potassium carbonate	10

(ii)		
	Potash feldspar	2.5
	Bone ash	17
	Dolomite	30
	Soda ash	2.5
	Potassium carbonate	12
	Whiting	31
	Quartz	4.4

These two formulae serve well to illustrate the differences that can occur in the composition of ash from different parts of the same tree.

3. The following formula comes from Tichane and is a simplified version 'which contains the essential ingredients for a simple synthetic ash':

Whiting	25
Dolomite	25
Potassium carbonate	12
Bone ash	5
Iron oxide	1

4. Joseph Grebanier, in his book *Chinese Ceramic Glazes*, gives us the following formula for what he calls his 'common' or mixed ash:

Bone ash	5
Whiting	36
Magnesium carbonate	7
Buckingham feldspar	25*
China clay	10
Flint	10
Soda ash	4
Manganese dioxide	1
Red iron oxide	3

* Buckingham feldspar is an American potash feldspar.

5. Andrew Holden quoted the following ash substitute and it formed the basis for the experiments by my student mentioned earlier.

Potash feldspar	10
Whiting	60
Talc	5
Bone ash	5
Ball clay	15
Quartz	5

This process of conversion can also be used for local stones and, just by way of interest, the following formulae are firstly for what Hamada calls Terayama Stone and secondly for Penlee Stone which formed the basis of Michael Cardew's black glaze.

(i)	Soda feldspar	2.5
	Dolomite	.25
	Whiting	.11
	China clay	51.18
	Quartz	45.55

As can be seen, this is a stone with a very high silica content. Indeed Hamada called it an impure quartz.

(ii)	Potash feldspar	37
	Magnesium carbonate	7.3
	Whiting	7
	Red iron oxide	10.73
	China clay	26.52
	Quartz	11.42

This is another stone high in silica but this time with a high proportion of iron. For the purposes of creating glazes with this material it can be regarded as a feldspar with iron and may only require further additions of wood ash or whiting to make a good glaze.

9 The glaze on these two bowls is made to the same formula, my standard ash glaze which you will find at the back of the book. The bowl on the left however, contains an ash substitute developed as described in the section on Synthetic Ashes. Although both samples require further adjustment (they are both too runny) you can see there is very little difference between them. The 'fake' ash glazed bowl is showing signs around the unglazed area of too much soluble alkali in the mixture. This, of course, is easily remedied.

A bucket form by Takeshi Yasuda, 10" high.
Takeshi Yasuda's work is living proof of two things, that pots of stunning quality can be made from 'reconstructed' ash glazes and that an oxidising atmosphere need never be a barrier to rich and exciting surfaces.

The glaze on this piece is a golden honey colour and the dark chocolate brown areas are manganous oxide mixed with a little of the glaze and applied with a brush.

Glaze:			
	Potash feldspar	20	
	Nephaline syenite	15	
	Whiting	20	
	Talc	10	
	China clay	15	
	Quartz	15	
	Bone ash	2	Manganese dioxide 0.15
	Red iron oxide	0.8	

Survey of some
Ash Glaze Potters

Two plates by the author. Largest 15" dia. Reduction fired 1280°C

Both of these plates are glazed with my standard ash recipe. The larger plate has beech ash in the recipe and the smaller one has walnut. As you can see from the photograph there is little difference between them. In reality the beech has a slightly bluer character than the walnut. If you look closely the soft, sweeping brush strokes in white slip can be seen under the glaze lending an extra dimension to the surface quality. The recipe for this glaze is at the back of the book.

Katherine Pleydell-Bouverie

It seems to me that any book that tries to document the development of ash glazes amongst Western 20th-century potters can hardly fail to include the work of Katherine Pleydell-Bouverie. At the time of writing this, it is some fifteen years since her passing but her contribution to the understanding and appreciation of this area of ceramics remains with us. Her copious and meticulous recordings of a lifetime's investigation into the effects of different ashes and the quiet, understated beauty of her pots remain as her legacy to potters and lovers of pottery throughout the world.

It has always been a matter of some regret to me that I never actually met K.P.B. and for that reason I feel somewhat inadequate in trying to describe her, as a woman, in relation to her work. Much has been written about her, and a little by her, that may give us some clues as to the character behind the pots. Richard Batterham, a friend for many years, said of her: 'She was a generous, constructive and supportive friend, positive without being dogmatic. She had an incisive, commonsense mind together with a lovely, slightly impish, full-flowering smile and a wink.'

Gentle, unassuming, quiet, yet not afraid to make a bold statement and a certain air of nobility, that intangible something that enables a person (or pot) to remain serene and yet not go unnoticed in a crowd. All these things would be said of K.P.B. and her pots. Of all the potters I have seen or known none are more epitomised in their work than she.

K.P.B.'s rather aristocratic background, her father was the fifth Earl of Radnor, makes her achievements in pottery even more remarkable. Katherine

never had to think in terms of 'earning a living' by her craft. She had a privileged, comfortable background. The sort of background that might have encouraged a young girl of some means to have become a socialite, never feeling either the need or desire to devote herself to a hard and often punishing craft, let alone to master it and make a truly giant contribution that would help shape its development for most of what remained of the century.

It wasn't until 1924 after having served in hospitals in France during the First World War and the almost compulsory three-year sojourn in London that she managed to persuade Bernard Leach to accept her as a pupil at his pottery in St Ives. When the year was finished she returned to the family home at Coleshill with Ada Mason (Peter) and Tsuranosuke Matsubayashi. It was Matsubayashi who had re-built the kiln at St Ives for Bernard Leach and had been responsible for much of K.P.B's. basic understanding of ceramic chemistry. Katherine, along with Michael Cardew and Ada Mason who had both shared here time at St Ives, would all sit around the eating table in the main part of the pottery each armed with notebook and pencil ready to try and make sense of 'a wild sort of pidgin English' that would sometimes send her into bursts of irrepressible laughter. 'Velly important the cray should have the plasty', he would say. 'For which put in tub with water till smell bad, yes leally strike your nose too much, when have the plasty and perfect conditions for make the cray body.'

In his autobiography Michael Cardew recalled how the only person who 'kept full and conscientious notes' was Katherine and how, much later on, when faced with technical problems in Africa, he had had to copy them from her. At Coleshill, Matsu, as he became affectionately known, designed and helped build a two-chambered, wood-fired kiln. The first chamber was for glazed stoneware, sometimes fired as high as 1400°C and the second chamber for biscuit or, with the help of some extra side stoking, for oxidised stoneware.

Inspired by a chance conversation with Bernard Leach about Chinese ash glazes, Katherine, Ada Mason and then in 1928 Norah Braden set about exploring the possibilities of glazes made from the various woods and plant ashes gleaned from the estate at Coleshill. She also took advantage of a number of local clays including an ochre, which together with ball clays and China clay from Devon and Cornwall made up the several clay bodies that were used simultaneously.

From the very beginning Katherine kept precise, if slightly idiosyncratic, records of each and every glaze test, often adding by way of a personal aide-mémoire a description that, for her, summed up the result, good or bad! 'Like black boot polish' was one less than impressed comment. 'Not bad, but a shade dull' was another, rather more encouraging evaluation. As a measure of the lengths to which Katherine would go to to ensure the accurate recording of her trials, she would record both the clay body (as an incised number) and the glaze (as a painted number, usually in Roman numerals) on the bottom of many of her pots. This habit, whether she intended it or not, provided future students with a clear record of the glaze on individual pots and made it possible for me to be able to include here the recipes for the pots shown in the colourplates.

The breadth and variety of surface and colour that Katherine achieved were quite amazing. The estate at Coleshill contained many different trees and shrubs and after pruning or felling by the estate woodmen, each wood was carefully gathered and segregated for burning. Apple, beech, box, thorn, elm, cedar, larch, spruce and walnut were among the trees that were tested. Laurustinus, rose, privet, chrysanthemum, honeysuckle and grass were amongst the shrubs and plants. From these came delicate crackled green celadons and dark, sombre blue-greens that almost became black. There were bright rust glazes that Katherine likened to chestnut and a wide range of cool, pale, off-whites sometimes with a crackle and sometimes with a matt, alabaster-like surface that lent themselves to brush decoration.

The years at Coleshill had, by and large, been successful but the Second World War and the blackout brought an end to potting. At first this was temporary, but with the peace came the realisation that Coleshill had become too big and difficult for Katherine to cope with its day to day management. Katherine moved to Kilmington Manor where she commandeered the huge barn as a workshop and she and Norah Braden built a new oil-fired kiln.

The change from wood to oil, by her own account, was a traumatic one:

Well, it was very silly, because neither of us knew anything about oil . . . we got too big a burner and too big a blower, so that the first time we fired just about everything blew up in the first ten minutes. Not sure if it was more funny than alarming, smoke belching out and pots going off like guns and all of us as black as sweeps.

Despite this hesitant beginning Katherine 'persisted in slightly uneasy fellowship' until, in 1960, she made a concession to her advancing years and installed an electric kiln for 'lower temperatures and an easy life'. From here on Katherine managed, by the judicious use of low temperature frits and mixtures of colouring oxides, to produce just as lively, interesting glazes in oxidation at lower temperatures as she had done previously. She continued to make stoneware in the great barn at Kilmington until her death in 1985 at the age of 89.

I would love to be able to finish this piece with a short, personal anecdote that would paint a succinct portrait of Katherine Pleydell-Bouverie. Unfortunately I cannot because, as I have said, I never met her. I do though, know people who did visit her, strangers to her, who were always welcomed with tea and cakes and who often left with pots given and not paid for. Every so often, but sadly not often enough, one finds a person that nobody has anything bad to say about — it seems that Katherine was one such person. Tales of her generosity, warmth and mild eccentricity are written by those who did know and love her and those same virtues are mirrored in her pots and thankfully I have a few of those.

Jar 4½″ tall

Below
Two cut-sided bowls

Below
Bulbous jar

Top page 86

This little jar is 4½″ high and was made in 1951. I know this because it has the date, the clay body number and perhaps more importantly for us at least, a number which refers to the glaze recipe all on the underneath. The glaze, described by K.P.B. as a grey but which I would describe as a soft, muted green is:

Potash feldspar	45
China clay	10
Frit*	10
Quartz	15
Mixed wood ash	20
Ball clay	10
Red iron oxide	1

*Katherine Pleydell-Bouverie often resorted to the use of a low temperature frit to bring down the maturation point of a particularly stubborn glaze. The frit mentioned in this recipe was a soft boracic glaze that contained lead. I would suggest trying this glaze without a frit at all at 1280°C but if you should like to try to stay as close to Katherine's recipe as possible, then perhaps a similar amount of calcium borate may be used as a substitute.
Author's Collection.

Page 86

Two cut-sided bowls, fine examples of the technique at which K.P.B. became so accomplished. She would often cradle a pot with fine lines carved into the outside or a deft fluting that would emphasise and enhance the form while at the same time providing a relief on which the ash glazes could perform their magic.
The bowl on the left is 4″ in diameter and has a glaze made from the ash of the box tree.

Box ash	20
Potash feldspar	20
China clay	10
Ball clay	10

It seems, from reading Katherine's notes, that this glaze requires at least 1300°C. The splash of colour at the rim is magnetic iron oxide.
The bowl on the right is 2¾″ in diameter and appears to have had an oxidised firing. The recipe for the glaze is:

Holly ash	50	
Whiting	30	
Potash feldspar	80	
Quartz	20	
China clay	40	
Ball clay	40	1260°C

Collection, University of Wales, Aberystwyth.

A large jar by Katherine Pleydell-Bouverie.
The thick, oily glaze has been brushed with an iron pigment to produce a variety of colour and texture. The glaze is made from the ash of the box shrub and is:

Box ash	35
Potash feldspar	55
Quartz	10
China clay	10

It is described by K.P.B. as a 'rather smokey grey'.

Page 87

The depth and quality of the glaze on this bulbous jar is wonderful. The colours, a mixture of Indian reds and ochres, are a typical response from a high lime glaze when iron oxide is brushed over it. The jar was made during the 1930s and the glaze recipe is:

Mixed wood ash	20
Potash feldspar	20
Quartz	20
China clay	10
Ball clay	20
Borax frit	7

A small reduction in the clay content would possibly render the frit unnecessary.
Collection, University of Wales, Aberystwyth.

Page 90

A small, faceted jar 5¼″ high. Although quite modest in size, the coolness of the glaze and the quiet austerity of the form give it a presence that belies its stature. I would guess that it was faceted at the leather hard stage and the cut lines probably softened a little before biscuiting. It appears that the crackle lines have been stained, possibly with ink, although I have no evidence that K.P.B. ever did this and the coloration may be due simply to age.

Wood ash	20
Potash feldspar	20
China clay	10
Ball clay	10

Collection, University of Wales, Aberystwyth.

Page 91

Not all of K.P.B.'s recipes contained wood ash and often she would take a formula and substitute wood ash for all or part of the limestone. This beautiful rounded bottle has a glaze for which the recipe is:

Potash feldspar	20
Quartz	20
Whiting	20
Ball clay	20

and appears to have been oxidised. The same recipe crops up later in her notes only this time the whiting has been replaced by walnut ash and produces a successful green celadon. I know from personal experience that walnut ash can be replaced with the more common beech or oak.
Collection, University of Wales, Aberystwyth.

Small faceted jar 5¼" tall

Rounded bottle

Phil Rogers

I am sure that writing this section about my own work is going to be the most difficult of all. Often, when one is very close to something its most endearing virtues can go unnoticed and a new, fresh set of eyes is required to fully appreciate any piece of work. Of the other potters featured in this book it was without exception that I noticed certain elements in their work that had hitherto gone unseen by themselves. This was not due to any great appreciative skills on my part or to any insensitivity on theirs, just that familiarity breeds contempt. I have often heard it said that a potter is never the best judge of his own work. It is certainly true that on many occasions other people have found virtue in pots that I have dismissed as failures. Professionalism dictates, though, that we must be our own worst critics and the final judgement must rest with the maker.

I went to art college in Newport and Swansea at the end of the 1960s. I was convinced that I was going to be a painter of some renown and even after the realisation came that this was not going to be the case, it took a little while before pottery became as important to me as it is now.

It wasn't that I made bad paintings, I even sold some of them! but I knew that I was never going to be really good. At the same time I definitely knew that somewhere there was an avenue of expression in which I could excel. It was waiting for me, all I had to do was find it.

While I was at college I played with pottery. We hadn't a lecturer in the college who really knew what studio pottery was about and we lurched from one disaster to another armed only with a copy of

Bernard Leach's *A Potter's Book* as guidance. A friend and I taught ourselves to throw, after a fashion, and we would have competitions as to who could throw the biggest pot regardless of shape only to discard these 'exercises' into the clay bin from whence they came. When my studies were completed I had mastered the technical difficulties of throwing but precious little else.

There then followed one of those strange twists of fate that often mould the rest of our lives. A teaching post took me to Cambridgeshire and the discovery, in Cambridge itself, of a craft gallery called Primavera, run in those days by Henry Rothschild. This was the first time that I had come across the work of potters which, until then, had merely been photographs in books or magazines. It was all there – Richard Batterham's ash-glazed pots alongside Ray Finch's Winchcombe domestic stoneware; standard ware from the Leach pottery; John Maltby's salt-glazed flagons, and Walter Keeler's tall, sensuous ash-glazed jugs. All these people were my teachers although they didn't know it. I spent many Saturday mornings just handling the pots, looking, trying to work out how things were done and then bit by bit trying to achieve the same standards of craftsmanship while all the time becoming more and more aware that a workshop and the chance to make pots every day were an inevitability.

At the time of writing this I have been a full-time potter for nearly thirteen years and if nothing else at least we have survived. At present my workshop is a converted stone 'cow-house' that overlooks the Wye Valley amidst the stunning countryside of mid-Wales. Another building houses the 75 cu. ft. oil-fired kiln which stands alongside the smaller salt-glaze kiln whilst yet another old barn contains the clay preparation area.

Mid-Wales is truly a wonderful place to live and the countryside around us affects the pots that I make in a number of ways. I try to use local materials as much as is practically possible and so there is a very strong and direct link here. Also, on the occasions that I decorate by drawing onto the pots, my motifs are lifted from my surroundings — plant forms and their fruits, fish in the river or the patterns made by flowing water all simplified to their very basic lines and executed swiftly and without hesitation in an attempt to get at the real essence of the subject.

I am truly fascinated by the work of the old country potters. Somehow, from amidst the every-day struggle of making a living from what was (some would say still is) a lowly paid craft there emerges a feeling of sheer effortlessness that belies the true labour that was spent in the making of these pots. Potters had to produce large numbers of pots just to survive and out of this very pressure of work came an unfussy and by their standards streamlined approach that we perceive as a relaxed softness. Only in our country pots have we Europeans ever achieved anything like the relaxed surety of the 15th-century Koreans for instance. I have tried, from the very beginning, to bring to my work a certain quality that speaks directly of clay and glaze in its most natural and obvious form.

My pots are thrown with soft clay and turned, when turning is necessary, quickly with the least amount of fuss, often leaving behind the marks of the turning tool in the still soft clay. They are thrown with the glaze in mind. This may seem a rather obvious statement but by it I mean that my glazes rely for their beauty on the lines and ridges that I apply to the spinning pot and those areas of relief that I add on later.

For my ash glazes to be at their best they require hollows into which to run and pool and in doing so produce magical changes of colour and texture. They like lines from which they flow away to leave dark, burnt edges that can highlight a shoulder or a rim. The pots are orchestrated to try to take full advantage of the flowing glaze, each mark and accent a considered decision.

In their making I am constantly trying to find new ways of treating the pot's surface so as to provide an interesting 'canvas' on which the glazes

can operate. Sometimes the form is derived out of a desire to execute a particular pattern. Certainly the making processes are often subordinate to a type of surface treatment such as the 'bashing' or beating of a pot when it may be necessary to be able to place a hand inside to support the wall of a bottle and then to throw the neck and lip as an addition later. Many of the pots are faceted, that is, they are thrown twice their normal thickness and then cut which creates lines that are highlighted by glaze and light. Some are lambasted in a thick white slip so that the brush marks show through the glaze coating, others are merely dipped into one of three slips that I use. These can alter both the colour of the glaze and its fired textural quality.

From the very beginning of my fascination for all things ceramic, it always seemed to me a good idea to try and use the materials around us to create our pots. It is certainly true that the pots that held the greatest attraction were those that displayed a direct and energetic approach in the making and, by their colour and surface quality, were saying something about an intimate relationship between the maker and his or her materials.

Page 94
Large jar, 26" high.
This jar or bottle was thrown in three sections. The new partly thrown collar was joined to the stiffened rim of the previous section and then thrown to a new height in readiness for the next section. The incised marks were made with a toothed wooden tool and the corner of an old hacksaw blade. The glaze is made from pine ash and is my most used, standard recipe. Pine is the one wood that I can obtain in very large quantities to heat our house. The recipe is as follows:

Pine ash	53
Cornish stone	14.5
Potash feldspar	14.5
China clay	6
Whiting	5
Quartz	7.25

I have used this as a basic recipe for a long time with many different types of wood ash. It often requires minor adjustments of the clay, feldspar or quartz depending on the fluxing power of the ash in question. As I have mentioned in the text of this book the body on to which you put your glaze will have a marked effect on the glaze quality. The body that I use is based on a Dorset ball clay and has a medium colour which encourages 'burning through' on edges and incised lines.

S.M.D. ball clay	25
Dobles fireclay	3
Feldspar	1.5
White silica sand 40's	1
Grog 60's	1
Red iron oxide	0.2

Two teabowls 4½″ high

Two boxes, largest 5″ diameter

It seems to me a great shame that recently we have seen a movement in ceramics that has trivialised skills and finds little merit in the understanding of the potter's materials. No longer, it seems, do we need to know how materials work, it suffices to know that they do. Being a 'potter' means more than this to me. It is no coincidence that the finest work in clay, irrespective of style and direction, nearly always displays the maker's obvious delight in and intimate knowledge of his materials. The serious and inquisitive potter should make it his or her business to investigate and thoroughly understand, if not the chemical intricacies then at least the working properties of the materials that create the effects that one chooses to obtain.

Wood ash seems to provide the perfect material to satisfy those requirements that are important to me as a potter. I get immense satisfaction in preparing and then using a glaze material that I can honestly claim as unique to me. I know that ashes can often be similar and ash glazes that I make can resemble ash glazes by other potters but this

knowledge does not diminish the feeling that I have of the individuality of my hard won material. It is interesting to read Bernard Leach on this subject in an extract from *Toward a Standard* written in 1940,

contact with the source in nature of his clay, pigment and glaze materials gives a potter more control and scope for the taking advantage of the variations which nature always offers. He should not want to

standardise, or to depend entirely upon those reliable but uninteresting substances which the potters merchant offers to the trade.

I was right, it has been difficult to write about myself. In short, the making of pots has become a kind of journey. Occasionally one can travel a long way in just one day and then sometimes, when things go wrong, the direction is backwards. I think it probably wise to say no more and let the pots speak for themselves and the viewer to decide upon their merit. For the finish I am mindful of Geoffrey Whiting's words, 'A potter is really not such a bad thing to be'.

Top page 95

Two teabowls, 4¼" high.

I love to make these small bowls; their scale means that they can be picked up and cradled easily in the hands. Because they are made quite quickly they lend themselves to a certain carefree attitude and I often find that I can achieve qualities on larger pots that I first discovered in the making of teabowls.

Both bowls have been thrown with a heavy ring around the middle with the intention of catching the fluid glaze. The pattern on the left was made with a clay stamp in the soft clay and on the right with a piece of window sash. Both have been dipped into a white slip of one-third Molochite and two-thirds SMD ball clay. The bowl on the right was then glazed with the straw ash glaze from the photograph on p. 33, a good example of how a different slip can radically alter the quality of a glaze. The bowl on the left has a beech ash glaze as follows:

Beech ash	50
Cornish stone	14
Potash feldspar	17.5
China clay	10
Quartz	8.75

Reduction fired 1280°C.

It is as well to repeat here that the ash quantities in my recipes may seem a little high. This is because I do not sieve the ash dry before washing. The amounts in the glaze batch allow for a certain amount of waste that will not pass through the 80's mesh sieve and is discarded. Potters who sieve away this residue before weighing into the glaze batch will have to adjust the ash quantity accordingly. Probably around 25% less.

Bottom page 95

Two boxes, the largest 5" diameter.

The box on the right has the same combination of slip and glaze as the bowls on page 95. The box on the left has a high silica ash glaze similar to Hamada's Nuka glaze and some Jun glazes from 13th-century China. In this case the glaze, which normally fires much lighter in tone, has been covered in a layer of red iron oxide banded over with a broad brush. The recipe is:

Feldspar	30
Local granite or basalt dust	30

(Seek out a quarry and ask for the fine airborne dust in the crushing sheds. The dust I use is a gritstone and is approximately 6% iron.) Replace with Cornish stone if unavailable and add around 1% iron to the total.

Ash	50
Quartz	40

Page 98

Bottle, 12" high.

This pot was thrown, in the first instance, only to a point just past the shoulder because I needed to be able to get my hand inside to support the walls as I 'bashed' the lattice pattern with a wooden tile at the soft leather hard stage. The top was added later as a coil and thrown on. The whole pot was then dipped into a slip made from a local ochre which I dig in the wood above the pottery and subsequently glazed with a straw ash mixture as follows:

Straw ash	59.5
Potash feldspar	21.5
China clay	3.5
Whiting	4.5
Talc	6
Quartz	5

Top page 99

Squared bowl, 10" diameter.

Squaring off any thrown shape dramatically alters the character of the pot. Horizontal lines suddenly become curved and create a wave movement around the piece. In this bowl I have left a heavy ring around the outside and on squaring, this line then follows the rim in its convoluted form. The inside has been brushed with a thick white slip hakeme' style which also adds to the movement of the bowl. The outside is glazed in a 'Tenmoku' made by adding 15 parts of whiting and 10 parts of feldspar to 70 parts of my local quarry dust. The inside glaze is the straw ash. (See reference to straw ash on page 32.)

Bottom page 99

A wide shallow dish, 12" diameter.

One of the benefits of using ash glazes is that they are particularly suitable for use in the salt kiln. The effects of the salt are to lighten the colour and to further flux the ash glaze which, on more upright shapes, can produce rivulets of glaze and a kind of 'kinetic' decoration. This dish has been glazed with a pine ash glaze on the inside only and the rim brushed with a slip made from porcelain clay which has salted to a pale orange/pink. The incised drawing was again done with the corner of my trusty hacksaw blade.

A large bottle by the Author, 14" high.
Beech ash glaze over a white slip. Reduction fired 1280°C.

Opposite
Bottle 12" high

Left
Square bowl

Below
Wide shallow dish

Mike Dodd

Knowing something of the sort of education that Mike Dodd experienced, I suppose it was almost inevitable that he should become a potter. He attended Bryanston School in Dorset where he was taken in hand by Donald Potter, a sculptor, potter and teacher who had been a student of Eric Gill.

The essence of Potter's teaching was to surround his students with fine examples of work by Leach and Cardew, both in the studio and on visits to exhibitions. He was introduced to Katherine Pleydell-Bouverie and visited the pottery, near Blandford, of Richard Batterham, who was another former pupil of Donald Potter. This constant exposure to fine pots and dedicated, almost obsessed, potters mixed with, what must have been a special kind of teaching, left their mark on Mike and although the decision to become a working potter wasn't taken until after a spell at Cambridge University, his approach to the craft, right from the very beginning, was one influenced by the pots he had become familiar with and the potters with whom he had talked.

While at Cambridge he was deeply impressed by some longquan pots at the Fitzwilliam Museum. Indeed he had been so deeply moved by the very presence of these pots that he likens their effect on his emotions to that which some people experience when listening to certain pieces of music — they quite literally brought tears to his eyes. This instinctive emotional reaction and the sense of enrichment that developed became the spur to abandon a promising career in medicine and to devote his life for the foreseeable future to pottery. Initially, Mike was interested in form and set about reproducing those shapes which he had seen that excited him. However, he soon came to realise that the form and its content were inexorably linked,

You can have someone make a good copy of a Bernard Leach pot and it can be a very good formal copy but it doesn't have the feel. So, essentially for me it's about your own feelings which you can't put into words but which you can put into a form because form is all we have. Pottery is a communication and communication is language. Pottery is a form of abstract language and anyone with the level of perception required to understand that language will feel the same feelings that I did when I first saw those pots in the Fitzwilliam.

He will tell you that his main concern in making his pots is that they should have dignity. By that I think he means that a pot needn't necessarily have importance in itself but rather one's pots, as a life's work, should reach out and say something about their maker through messages in their form and their glaze, in the way that a footring is turned or a handle is terminated. 'Some potters are clay people, some are flame people and some are glaze people and when you get them all together in one, then you have a Hamada or a Bernard.'

It is little surprise then, considering his background, that Mike Dodd's work with ash in his glazes has become a logical extension of his fascination with the use of the rocks, clays and silts that he finds, in some abundance, around his home in Cumbria, a little to the south of the Scottish border. This is the site of Mike's fourth pottery, the previous three having all been in the south of England. As with all the others, Mike's great concern and joy is creating stoneware glazes of great beauty and individual character from those materials on his doorstep. To this end he carries out an endless series of experiments, the success or failure of one leading to the next trial and then to the next and so on ever mindful of Hamada's assertion that to work closely and intimately with a limited number of materials and glazes is really the only way to develop a truly individual style.

By carefully utilising the granites, andesites and hornfels quarried in the area with the ochre from the bank of a stream and an iron deposit that leaches, bright orange from the side of a hill and combining all these with a selection of different wood ashes, willow and hawthorn in the main, Mike has developed a series of glazes that are amongst the most exciting ever seen in this country. Probably the most important feature of these glazes are that they belong to Mike alone, partly because of decisions that he has made along the way but mostly because he has used the materials close to him. This avenue of almost limitless exploration is open to anyone — it only requires the commitment and a determination that one's glazes should speak of oneself and not of another.

The wood ash that Mike Dodd uses in his glazes comes from three main sources. The mixed wood ash comes from the fire in his own house. It is a variable mixture and is accepted on those terms; the glaze in which it is used (an old Leach standard) being less dependent on the type of ash because the ash content is not so high. The hawthorn is the result of keeping a careful eye open for farmers burning off the branches after a session of hedging but it is the willow ash that should be added to our list of unusual sources. The ash is the waste product from the burning of offcuts at a cricket bat factory!

One or two of the glazes are used on their own, placed directly over the clay body, a dark burning mixture of iron-bearing ball clay and a sand-bearing clay from Cornwall. However, just as often they are used in conjunction with a slip underneath. A white slip made from ball clay and Molochite is used to lighten the colour of the top glaze. I use this same slip myself and find that a difference in the surface quality of the glaze can also be expected; sometimes changing what would have been shiny areas into a surface that can resemble smooth marble. Mike also uses an ochre that he digs locally which contains quite a high iron content. Underneath a glaze, this slip will tend to darken the colour and also provide a rich under-surface to reveal with deft strokes

through the still wet glaze layer. The iron that I spoke of earlier, which leaches out of the ground and settles in a local river, provides a rich, kaki-like covering, and another local iron-bearing stone when used alone as an overdip makes a beautiful lustrous iron glaze reminiscent of the kaki glaze of Mashiko.

If I am honest I would have to declare a bias because Mike Dodd makes the sort of pots that first awoke my interest in pottery, although at that time the pots that I had seen were made by Bernard Leach, Hamada and then Richard Batterham. Having said that, I firmly believe that Mike Dodd is making some of the most exciting work ever seen in this country. His latest work shows a consummate understanding not only of his materials but also of the complicated relationships of form, colour and decoration expressed with that controlled freedom that is only available to someone totally in command of his craft, only the kiln is left to have the last say.

Left
Faceted bottle

Below
Two store jars

Page 102

A thrown and squared dish, 9" across.

This dish has been made square after being thrown and then covered with a white slip. The slip was then combed and lastly the pattern of grasses drawn through the slip to reveal the body below. The pale green ash glaze is:

Potash feldspar	40
Willow Ash	40
HVAR ball clay	20

It has been fired to 1300°C in Mike's 70 cu. ft. oil-fired downdraught kiln.

The combination of the hakeme technique and the drawing over the top has created a pattern with a wonderful sense of movement.

Top page 103

This tall, faceted bottle is 14" tall and carries a thick, creamy ash glaze similar to Hamada's Nuka glaze in that it contains a high proportion of silica. Indeed it is the surplus of silica undissolved in the melted glass that gives the glaze its opacity. This bottle, although relatively modest in scale, has a monumental feel.

Bottom page 103

Two storejars, part of Mike Dodd's range of domestic pots, the tallest being 9" tall.

Again these pots have been dipped in the white slip and then the combed patterns cut through this coating while it was still quite damp. The lines, impressed in the pots from top to bottom, although simply done, radically alter the whole feel of the pots and create a lobed effect. The semi-matt ash glaze used over the white slip is made from hawthorn ash and is as follows:

Potash feldspar	40	
Hawthorn ash	40	
Hyplas 71	10	(a high silica ball clay)
Whitehaven yellow clay	10	1300°C

The Whitehaven yellow clay may be substituted by a high iron ball clay such as AT or any local red clay or pale burning ochre. You may achieve a colour difference but so what!

Top page 106

A pitcher, 12" in height.

On this pot the glaze was applied directly over the clay body with no slip underneath. The ash glaze has run and pooled in the hollows of the decoration and thereby highlighted them, even creating its own linear decoration near to the base of the pot. This, not totally expected, 'extra' is an example of what I meant in the text about the kiln having the last say. The glaze is as follows:

Granite	5
Hornfels	5
Mixed ash	10
Hyplas 71	4

The dark olive green colour of the glaze is derived from a quantity of iron contained in one or both of the stones.

Bottom page 106

Two teabowls or Yunomi.

Each has been faceted and the bases turned in a vigorous and lively fashion. The bowl on the left has the creamy glaze over which has been laid a covering of iron. The other has the granite and hornfels glaze with an overdip of another glaze over the rim. The kiln has seen to the rest!

Page 107

A bottle, 11" high.

The ash in the underglaze on this pot plays much less of a role in the fired quality of the glaze than, for instance, the glaze on the pitcher. In this case the ash is something of a modifier, lending a subtle warmth and softness to a glaze that has a textural quality akin to alabaster, typical of a glaze containing talc. The pattern has been brushed with a wax resist and the top covering is pure iron from the natural deposit spoken of earlier. The glaze is:

Cornish stone	400
Whiting	20
Hyplas 71	180
China clay	40
Talc	40
Mixed wood ash	100

One handled bottle, 26 cm high. Hawthorn ash glaze over dark slip with fingerwipe decoration.

A pitcher

Below
Two teabowls

Opposite
A bottle

Eric James Mellon

Eric James Mellon had always planned on being an artist. One of his earliest memories, at seven years of age, is of his uncle drawing and the wonderment that those pictures stirred within him. Later, at thirteen, he attended Watford Art School (1939–1944) and he vividly remembers the antique plaster figures, the stuffed animals in their cases and the smell of oil paint in the studios. For five years he studied life drawing, anatomy, composition and architecture; trained by academicians to draw and paint in watercolour and oil. From 1945 until 1950 he studied book production and illustration at the Central School of Art in London while at the same time studying pottery at Harrow School of Art. In 1951 he, his wife, the painter Martina Thomas, and amongst others, the potter Derek Davis, set up a community to draw and paint and make pottery.

Eric Mellon's pots are unlike the work of anyone else working in this country at present. He combines a considerable talent as a graphic artist with the skills necessary to create ceramic pieces of such charm and humour that the complexities of thought and great seriousness of message sometimes go unnoticed while the eye plays games, skipping over the story packed surfaces unable to rest for too long before darting to a previously unseen detail. Mellon's pots are the vehicles for his decoration.

Eric Mellon has two places of work. His studio at home which he calls his think-tank and a studio and workshop at Slindon College in Sussex where he is Director of Art Studies. When I visited him he took me to both places. The studio at Slindon College is a tall Georgian room with huge windows that allow masses of daylight to flood to all corners. This is where Mellon draws the figure, employing a number of models who pose, not only for Mellon himself, but for some of the pupils under his tuition. These periods of concentrated study are crucial to him as an artist not only providing the vocabulary for his extensive repertoire of painted imagery but feeding an insatiable desire to get to the essence of the human figure.

The studio at home in Bognor Regis speaks more than a little about the man. There is little room to move. Almost every usable space harbours either the fruits of Mellon's own prodigious creativity or pots from other potters whom he admires. Drawings and mounted watercolours stand in rows on the floor and filing cabinets are testament to Mellon's professionalism. He keeps in them papers relevant to himself and his work and can produce any given paper in seconds.

On both sides of this studio rows of shelves have pots crammed onto them. In amongst his own work, both recent and earlier, there are, surprisingly, a lot of pots that seem to spring from the Leach tradition. Batterham, Mommens and Denis Moore are represented and also Sarah Walton. Seth Cardew's pots and one by Henry Hammond sit next to work that traces Mellon's own developement as a decorator, potter and student of wood ash as a glaze material since 1965.

For Eric Mellon the pots are the final statement and coming together of many things. His figure drawing in pencil and with brush and the monotype prints lay the foundation for his watercolours which in turn form the pieces of the jigsaw that eventually appear on the pots. However, this only tells half the story. W.A. Ismay, in an assessment of Eric Mellon's work written in 1986, traces the progression of his decorative motifs from the early 1960s onwards. Painting based on observation of a peacock's tail or a particular flower or a horse and rider image gave way to a circus theme which included acrobats and trapeze artists. Commemorative pieces and portrait work (including one of William Ismay on receiving his MBE, and another to celebrate his eightieth birthday) and pieces containing social and political comment all contain a common strand, a narrative. Eric Mellon is a story teller.

The themes most continuous and fruitful are those of mythology. Interpretations of the story of Daphne and Apollo occupied him throughout the 1970s and then, towards the end of the decade, the three sons of Saturn, Jupiter, Neptune and Pluto. All of these themes provided immense scope for Mellon's lively imagination and fanciful sense of humour. Recently he has concerned himself with a theme he calls Tenderness. Here Mellon has explored that deepest emotion that can exist between two people. Not physical love; he directs his, and our, attention to the metaphysical. Lovers, naked, touch fingertips or float, Chagall-like, above the earth as if held in weightlessness by some unseen hand.

Slowly, Mellon has created his own mythology. A world of personal symbolisms together with elements borrowed from ancient myths and some lifted from modern literature such as *The Third Policeman* by Flann O'Brien and *The Little Prince* by Antoine de Saint-Exupéry. It includes bird maidens and moon goddesses, foxes and lions. The fox symbolises good fortune and the lion a new beginning or rebirth.

Mellon's mastery of the use of space, either within a bowl or around the belly of a pot is his genius. What could easily become a scramble of shapes and images is orchestrated into a visual poem that skips lyrically around a form. Often he will continue a figure over the edge of a bowl so that the legs may continue underneath. Sometimes, as with the series on mermaids, figures can encircle the underneath of a bowl only to finish within the footring. Lines and edges are no barriers to his imagination as neither are perspective nor relative scale. The insides of taller, more enclosed bowls and cylinder vases are also painted. Mellon's pots cry out to be picked up or walked around and read as with the pages of a book.

The forms that carry Mellon's huge vocabulary of decorative motifs are limited in number. There are bowls of various proportions, with the wide, shallow ones greatest in number. There are fat, globular bottles, sometimes with and sometimes without a footring underneath, and tiny vessels akin to the oriental teabowl but which Mellon sees as magical objects in much the same way as I regard the 'teabowl', a feeling that, for me at least, stems from the intimate scale of these pots. Probably the most majestic of his pots are the very tall, cylindrical bottles that flare outwards at the neck, sometimes almost two feet in height.

Eric Mellon's fascination with wood ash glazes began through a desire to find richer surfaces for his oxide painting which would not destroy the drawings that he had put onto the pot. Most of the following comes directly from Eric Mellon's own notes.

Research into ash glazes was started in an effort to find richer glazes and many ashes were tested including pine, willow, elm, apple, pear, blackcurrant, cypress, beech and horse chestnut but the difficulties experienced with the bleeding of oxide-drawn lines led to frustration. A chance sample of privet ash which produced a glaze that didn't bleed the cobalt lines led him to question the difference between tree ashes such as elm or beech and bush ashes.

There is a difference between tree and bush ashes. Trees take calcium from the soil and grasses and bushes take silica. Therefore bush ashes provide strong glass formers in the glaze while tree ashes provide strong fluxes. Most of my glazes do not contain calcium other than that provided by the wood ash, because the decorating oxides are often fluxes and any added flux to the glaze will result in the brush drawing bleeding in the firing once high temperature has been reached. It took about ten years of careful study and testing to understand these principles before I could overcome the technical difficulties of the colouring oxides causing the glaze to collapse. I was then able to become a decorator of ceramics at high temperature allowing the beautiful qualities which can be achieved using ash glazes.

It is interesting to note here the way in which Eric Mellon applies his drawing to the pot. All the painting is done underglaze. He uses, for the most part, the pure oxides. Cobalt is used alone and then mixed 2 parts with 1 part of black copper oxide to give a blue. Iron oxide is used to obtain a red-brown which seems to glow in its lustrous quality. Body stains are used as an underglaze pigment, tan pink,

Inside and underside of bowl

Wide shallow dish

turquoise blue, blue grey, apple green and orange/red. Both the stains and the oxides are sometimes mixed with a single drop of gum arabic to help them adhere to the biscuit-fired pot and to prevent them from smudging or becoming airborne for reasons of health safety.

For Mellon, the new found ability to hold crystal clear the lines that he had drawn was a miracle. He had discovered that by balancing exactly the silica content of the glaze, the extra flux provided by the colouring oxides wasn't enough to break down the silica network and therefore the glaze didn't collapse.

From 1978 onwards only bush ashes have been used (with the exception of elm ash which Mellon continues to use for a small proportion of pots where he requires a softer edge to the decoration) and since 1979 he has used the ash from the Philadelphus bush for which he has an ongoing supply. This ash can be used to make excellent,

stable glazes firing as high as 1320°C. Latterly, with the help of his assistant, Mabel Padfield, he has also made use of the Escallonia as a source of ash.

When I visited him he showed me pots that illustrated all the qualities that I have written about. Drawings that showed a wonderful sureness of line reminiscent of Matisse or Hockney, with an understanding of the orchestration of shapes within a space rivalled only, in the contemporary scene, by John Maltby. The colours on his pots sing. The blue is strong and intense but never garish and the browns are rich and deep, like the skin of a newly opened chestnut. They can be well-defined with a hard edge and they can, depending on the ash in the glaze, be soft and dreamy. At its best Eric Mellon's work has that rare quality that transcends time and period. His magic and his poetry intermingled with a gentle eroticism create images that linger long in the memory.

Page 110

The inside and underside of a bowl, Theme of Tenderness,
Elm ash glaze. 9¼" diameter. 1987.

This bowl is a fine example of Eric Mellon's ability to create movement and pattern with figurative elements. The figures on the underside seem to float around the bowl whilst, on the uppermost side, the clever use of figures linked across a dark to light divide and a playful approach to perspective again create a strong feeling of movement as the eye is transported around and around, never quite knowing where to stop. The bowl is glazed with an elm ash glaze of:

Elm ash	40
Potash feldspar	40
China clay	25
Stoneware clay	5
(a pale ball clay would probably substitute here)	
Flint	10

Reduction fired to 1300°C.

The colours are applied with a brush and are a mixture of oxides and glaze stains.

Page 111

A wide shallow dish, one from a series depicting scenes from
the circus, 10½" diameter. 1970.

The wonderfully rich colours of this dish are typical of the kind of colour response one might expect from the application of the oxides of iron and cobalt to an ash glaze. Notice the clever use of perspective as the horse steps over the formal border and immediately creates a feeling of depth in the dish.

The glaze on this piece is the same as that on the bowl in plate 1 although I would guess fired slightly hotter and oxidised.

Page 114

Bottle, 7" high, Theme of Tenderness. 1986.

The higher silica content of this Philadelphus ash glaze has produced a glaze much less prone to running after the application of the colouring oxides.

Philadelphus ash	16	
Mixed feldspar	16	
China clay	10	
Ball clay	2	
Flint	9	1300°C

Collection of Eric Mellon.

Page 115

Two Bowls, Theme of Musicians, Both 7¼" diameter.

This photograph illustrates how Eric Mellon can carry a design over the edge of a bowl and around the underside even to the point of using the space under the footring as an integral part of the whole painting. A more clear comparison of two ash glazes can also be seen. The top bowl, with its softer slightly more diffused edges has the more lime-rich elm ash glaze. The lower bowl, with its crisper, cleaner appearance has the higher silica Philadelphus ash glaze.

Opposite

Bowl with a mermaid embracing a fox watched by the moon
goddess. Glaze made with Philadelphus ash.

Below

Eric Mellon decorating a bowl with preliminary drawings,
watercolours, monotypes and drawing books.

Top
Watercolour

Bottom
Bottle 'Tenderness'

114

Two bowls

Jim Robison

It would be easy to say that the reason why Jim Robison's most important works are large in scale is because he is an American. There is an element of truth here. Americans do seem to have a more expansive sense of what is or isn't large or small than we British, trapped, as we are, on an island whose tallest mountain is a mere pimple by comparison and our longest river just a dribble. Just as important though, in terms of Jim's sculptural ceramics, is his Yorkshire home. The hills and valleys around his Holmfirth studio provide a rich and varied source of visual material which he translates to the clay in his own very individual style. He seems to have taken that way that Americans have of thinking big, of not letting mere practical consideration get in the way of the true expression of the idea, and combined it with the intimate nearness of the Yorkshire Dales, with all its colours and textures.

Jim Robison was born in 1939 in Independence, Missouri and graduated, first of all with a BA in Fine Art from Graceland College in Iowa and then an MA in Sculpture and Ceramics from Eastern Michigan Univeristy. All this was after four years in the United States Air Force. Seven years of high school teaching in the States (where he met his future Yorkshire-born wife) was followed by a secondment to Wetherby High School. Jim is now an adopted son of Yorkshire and has become a Yorkshireman in everything but accent.

In understanding Jim's work one has to appreciate fully the love he has for the South Yorkshire landscape and all that it contains – its rocks and crags, its dry stone walls and lichen-covered gateposts, the patterns on the landscape and the folklore, the remnants of pre-history and the marks left by man over the years, some accidental, some deliberate. All these things have their part in Jim's interpretation of his surroundings. When one takes into account his American upbringing and his Fine Art background and even his time in the USAF, the pieces of the jigsaw begin to come together and the total picture emerges.

Although Jim does make a small range of wheel-thrown domestic pots, it is for his sculptural work that he is best known and it is this work that he considers to be, by far, his most important. He began handbuilding with clay while at college under the tutelage of Les Wight, and he lists Fred Bauer alongside Paul Soldner and Peter Volkous as his most powerful influences. He has examples of both Soldner's and Bauer's work at his home and revels in their free, unfettered use of the material. Soldner's work has a particular fascination in that the low temperature salt glaze typical of Soldner's most recent work is similar in colour and texture to Jim's high-fired stoneware pieces glazed with wood ash glazes.

In constructing his pieces, Jim's first step is to roll out large slabs by the use of an old, Victorian clothes mangle. He has devised a method of sandwiching pieces of clay between two lengths of hessian, all resting on a sheet of hardboard. This whole arrangement is then passed between the rollers. The resulting sheets of clay provide the starting point for many of his pieces. Firstly they are placed into curved formers where they may stay for anything up to three days until they are firm enough to proceed to the joining stage. Having been dried resting on a concave former, the sheet of clay now has the strength to support itself and has been transformed from a simple two-dimensional plane into a complex three-dimensional surface. Two of these sheets joined together immediately produce the vital characteristics of a vessel, a volume or space contained within a wall. Jim, however, doesn't see his work in terms of the vessel. Yes, they have a wall and a base but these are practical necessities to overcome the problem of firing large pieces. Jim would, I'm sure, quite like his pieces to be solid if it were possible. He is at great pains to create the illusion of solidity, of massiveness, of great weight — that monumental serenity one is aware of when one looks up at a craggy outcrop on the summit of a hill.

Jim even manages to use the mangle creatively and not just as a labour-saving device. He will roll and then reroll clay encouraging it to tear and split at the edges. Sometimes a piece of clay, having been rolled once, will be slipped and then the slip will be combed or drawn through before being rolled again. This time two sheets are rolled together and the combed, slipped area may show shrough a torn hole in the uppermost slab. If he's lucky the tears and splits form complex textures that belie the basic simplicity of their creation. Often, by the clever use of the machine and by a mixture of forethought and spontaneous improvisation, these holes or windows can reveal a pattern that can spread itself right across a piece but be revealed only where the top layer allows it to be seen. This creates both continuity and rhythm, a movement where the eye skips from one area to the next eager to seek the next point where the underlying strata are revealed as if by the erosion of the top layer.

Once the piece has been stood up and joined together with coils and the usual methods of welding clay together, additional slabs can be added on to it. Here is where the character of each piece really begins to show itself. Often, quite complicated constructions, usually geometric in nature, reminiscent of the crystal structures found in geology or the stratification of rock, sit proudly on the pinnacle. These geometric symbols are often echoed on the sides of a piece. This time they represent the marks that man has left behind on the landscape and are drawn into the soft clay and then inlaid with different coloured slips. These slips are coloured with various oxides. Cobalt and copper for the blue, iron and manganese for the brown and a pure porcelain slip for the white. The lines are then smoothed down when dry by the use of wire wool.

This method results in a clean, crisp line that couldn't really be achieved in any other way. Further applications of slip eventually build up layers of colour and by the selective rubbing away of coatings, a rich patina develops that eventually influences the colour of the covering coat of glaze.

It's important to note here that while rubbing down the slips with wire wool and when applying the sprayed glaze coat, Jim always wears a respiratory mask to avoid any inhalation of airborne dust.

Spraying is really the only practical method by which these, sometimes enormous, pieces can be glazed. At one time Jim worked with a man who sprayed cars and trucks for a living and he feels that the skills learned then have proved invaluable for his work in ceramics.

For his glaze, Jim uses a basic wood ash recipe which is a simple mixture of wood ash and clay. In strict terms this isn't really a glaze at all in that it doesn't melt. It is, I suppose, a refractory coating that contains very little silica, not enough to form a true glass. It is an extreme version of a high alumina matt. What it does do however, is to create the most wonderfully rich colours by the addition of small percentages of colouring oxides.

Jim had no real philosophic reason for beginning his work with wood ash glazes. At the time he was motivated by the burning of huge quantities of elm wood at Bretton Hall College where he is in charge of Sculpture and Ceramics. Later he came to know a sawmill where large amounts of branch wood were burnt every day. He also naively thought, as probably we all do at first, that this was a free material just there for the using. He did find though, that wood ash provided exactly the rich, earthy colours combined with the sort of textural qualities that were right for his work. He says that for the type of glaze that he uses he has never really noticed any appreciable difference from one wood ash to another. His glaze seems to work as well with elm ash, the mixed ash from the sawmill or other odd mixtures he has come by over the years.

In glazing the pieces, Jim works his way through a sequence of applications of the same base glaze but each with differing amounts of colouring oxides. First, a coat of the ash glaze containing 5%—10% of iron oxide is sprayed over the slips that were applied before biscuiting. Particular attention is paid to the textural qualities formed in the clay during the rolling. Tears or creases at the edges of the pieces or angular sections in the modelling are given careful consideration and may be sprayed two

Jim in Yorkshire

Below
Detail of vase on page 119

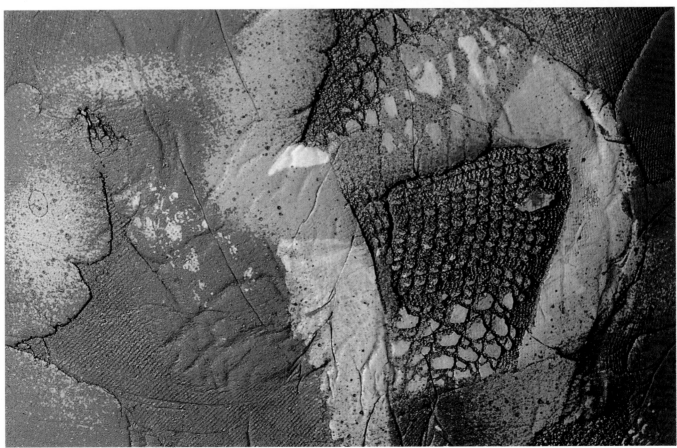

Two vases

or three times, selectively, in order to build up a strength of colour in certain places.

Having finished the first layer, Jim then sprays a new coating of the same base glaze but this time it contains a mixture of cobalt and copper. Again he pays great attention to the edges of the piece. Using the spray gun as an air brush, he will highlight those areas where he requires a rich ochre, sometimes using cardboard stencils to mask a shape or to create the effect of a shadow cast by a prominent part of the piece. Another glaze, not containing wood ash but with a small proportion of tin oxide, is used over those areas that have the white porcelain slip. The copper in the ash glaze flashes this pale buttery glaze to a pink.

All the pieces are fired in a reduction atmosphere to around 1280°C in a kiln that Jim built himself, and the finished works are testament to the man's considerable talent as a manipulator of clay and glaze. The creation of such large pieces of work on a regular basis takes courage. There is so much that can go wrong when the pieces are committed to the fire but usually nothing does. The enjoyment he derives from the constructional challenges of such large-scale work stands him in good stead and more often than not the work comes from the kiln without blemish.

Above all, Jim Robison's work has presence. In a room his pieces command the space around them and demand a certain reverence from the viewer. His approach to the use of wood ash is simplistic in the extreme. One base glaze in different batches with varying oxide constituents provides an almost infinite variety of colour and tone. It is the complex and masterly way in which he uses this simple combination that has become the hallmark of his work.

Glaze, slip and colouring details

Ash Glaze

Elm ash	10 lbs
China clay	9 lbs
Potash feldspar	2½ lbs
Whiting	2½ lbs

This glaze was initially a simple 50/50 mixture of ash and China clay but Jim came to consider this too dry. In preparing the ash, it is first added to the water, and then sieved though a 40's mesh to remove any large lumps and then through an 80's sieve. The ash is then left to dry ready for use.

All the different shades of brown and ochre are achieved by small additions of iron oxide in its various forms to the base glaze. For the blue/greens Jim uses a mixture of cobalt and copper (approximately 1.5% addition for the cobalt and 6.5% for the copper).

A thin coat of a feldspathic glaze is applied over the porcelain-slipped areas to increase the contrast in colour and texture. The glaze has a smooth buttery feel and gently flashes pink when placed near to the copper/cobalt ash glaze. The glaze is as follows:

Potash feldspar	29.5
Nephaline syenite	29.5
China clay	11.0
Whiting	13.5
Dolomite	3.0
Zinc oxide	3.0
Bentonite	.5
Zircon	5.0
Tin oxide	5.0

Occasionally small additions of body stains are added to this glaze if a particular colour is required.

Most of Jim's work is biscuit-fired except for the very largest pieces and then reduction-fired over 12 hours in his 40 cu.ft. propane-fired kiln.

page 119

Two large vessels, height 2' 3". These two imposing pieces display quite clearly the various sources of ideas that Jim Robison utilises in his sculptural pots. The landscape and all the shapes, colours and textures it contains, including man's contributions, are brought together and orchestrated to form a brief but comprehensive statement that is also a declaration of love and understanding of his surroundings.

Here we can see the results of sprayed layers of dry ash glaze. As layers build up so the colour changes from the chocolate brown which is the base coat through to a rich, glowing ochre. The areas of combed white slip help to create an impression of space and distance disappearing as they do, without hesitation, behind the strong dark colours in front.

Notice also the use of the imprinted texture (from different pieces of open weave cloth) and creases in the clay, the result of judicious manipulation of the clay sheets as they pass between the rollers of a large Victorian mangle.

page 122

A large open dish or plate, 14" across.

This piece is constructed from five slabs of clay that have been rolled out in the same way as for the larger constructed pieces. The central portion has, prior to rolling, been covered in the porcelain slip and the patterns combed through. The edges have been sprayed with the ash glaze with an increasingly thicker layer towards the edge nearest the central section. The combed porcelain slip has been glazed with the feldspathic glaze over a thin application of ash glaze that contains a small percentage of copper oxide.

Page 123

Two flat wall pieces. 12" across.

Jim has employed the same techniques in these two pieces. Although they are essentially flat in construction, there is a strong feeling of depth in the pattern and a sense of movement across the surface.

Large piece by Jim Robison

Jim uses a basic wood ash recipe which is a simple mixture of wood ash and clay. By the addition of small percentages of colouring oxides to his glazes, he creates the most wonderfully rich colours. Jim's method of using tears and creases and layers of glazes can be clearly seen above.

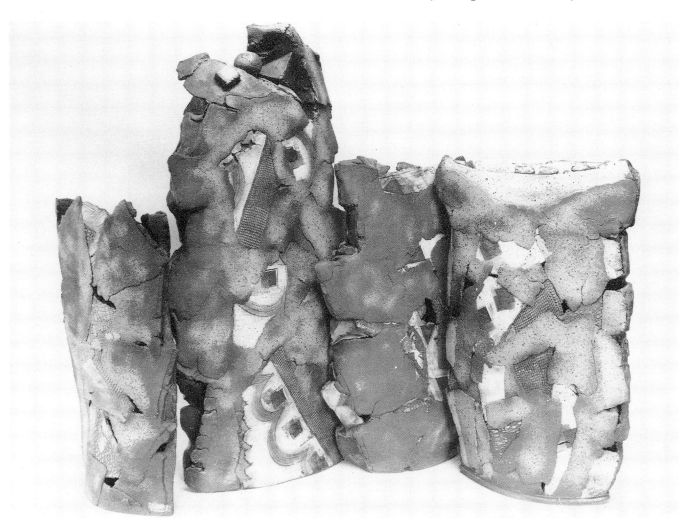

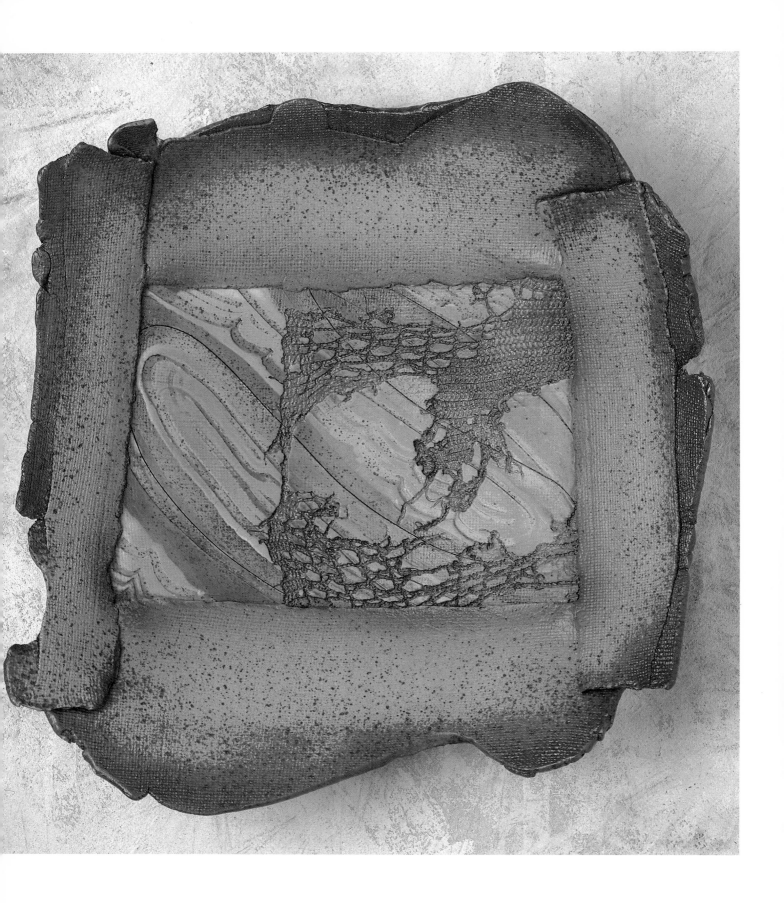

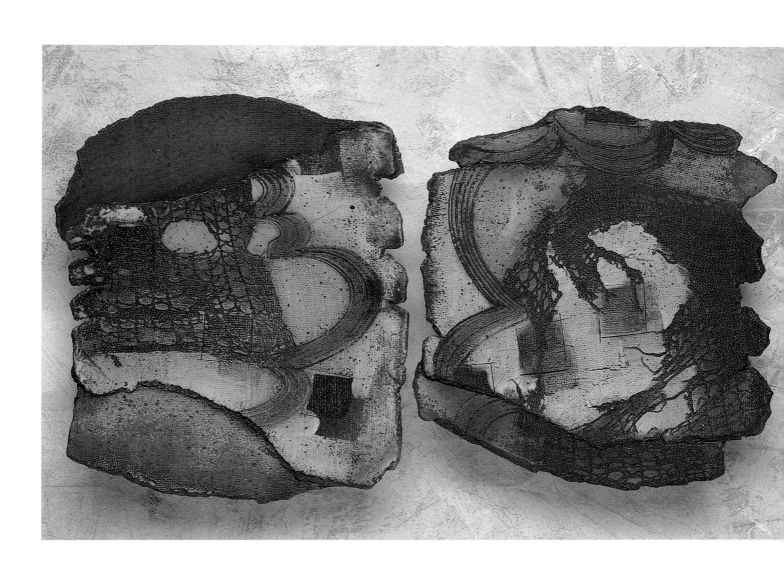

Left
Open dish

Above
Two wall plates

Tom Turner

I am a potter who loves pottery, old and new, along with the challenges, rewards and lifestyle of producing for a living. My work deals with the classical considerations of material, process and form and follows the 'more is less: less is more' philosophy. For me a beautiful form is more important than a painted decoration, whether it be a new pot or a 19th-century salt-glazed jug. It is my intention that these concerns are reborn in a contemporary and personal way through my work, maybe not in each individual piece, but as a body of work that represents a working life. In short, the personal refinement of a few basic pottery notions. Function is determined by the imagination of the owner of my work. A teapot can serve any liquid, hot or cold, or its function may be visual appreciation, which for me is the greatest function.

Tom Turner graduated from Illinois State University in 1968 and apart from two years US Army service has made pots ever since. In 1976 he resigned his full-time university lectureship to devote all his working time to the making of his pottery. He is currently working with his wife, potter Gail Russell, in the countryside just outside Delaware, Ohio in an old post and beam barn built around 1920 that they have called Peachblow Pottery. Although rural in its location Tom was careful to choose a place not too far from the city as he finds the cultural contact important to him. As a result his pottery lies only 20 minutes north of Columbus, the state capital.

Tom's fascination with wood ash began during his undergraduate studies at Illinois because of the visual and physical textures that develop by themselves during firing. From the beginning he found that it was the ability of wood ash to project its inherent character in the fired glaze that attracted him. Out of this respect for the material has developed a unique style of decoration that relies on the coaxing of the glaze surface into patterns without recourse to obvious or brutal persuasion. Instead, a rather gentle assistance is lent to magnify or slightly exaggerate the sort of textured surface that one might expect from the wood ash glazes.

All of Tom's work is in porcelain and fired in a 45 cu.ft. trolley kiln of his own design and build, which is fuelled with natural gas. Firings take approximately 14 hours and all of the pots are biscuit-fired in an electric kiln prior to glazing. In the glost fire, reduction is commenced at cone 06 (990°C) and proceeds until cone 8 is half over, then the reduction is lessened until cone 10 just touches. On completion the damper is closed but the burner ports are left open until the unpacking three days later.

The porcelain body was formulated by Tom in 1975 and is filter pressed from a slip produced in a large fibreglass tank. The shaft that carries the mixing blades is stainless steel, the pump is aluminium and rubber and the press plates and frames are aluminium so that no iron can possibly contaminate the porcelain. Tom maintains that the body is extremely throwable, translucent when thin and very white with only a minimum shrinkage. The recipe is as follows:

*Veegum T	16
(in the UK we would use a white bentonite)	
Old Mine *4 Ball Clay	
(UK possibly Hy-plas 71)	50

Georgia Kaolin Tile 6	300
Georgia Kaolin Kaopaque 20	150

(Tom suggests for a UK equivalent that Grolleg China clay may be substituted for the total combined weight of the Tile 6 and the K-20)

200 mesh quartz	300
Potash feldspar (FFF)	250
Epsom Salt (magnesium sulphate)	
Deflocculant	1

For the ash glazes Tom prefers whenever possible to use apple ash because he finds that of all the ashes this one gives him the best colour response although he often uses oak ash or a mixture of hardwood ashes from the wood burner that warms the house. The ashes are gathered and then sieved dry down to a 30's mesh. This is a process I prefer not to go through but, if it is carried out, I would strongly recommend the use of an efficient dust mask. To cut down wastage, the residue that doesn't pass through the sieve is crushed with a rolling pin and then resieved. Tom never washes his ash. He believes that the soluble fluxes are crucial to the character of each ash.

Most of his ash recipes are based on Leach's 4.4.2. mixture of:

40 Feldspar, 40 Ash, 20 Ball Clay

The type of ash, how it was burned, how it was sieved or processed, the type of feldspar and the types of clay give an abundance of variables to produce the different colours and textures.

Tom also uses what he calls a 'fake ash' glaze but what I would prefer to call an 'ash-like' glaze because it is a glaze type in its own right. The glaze is a combination of Albany slip, whiting and China clay. For UK potters the Albany slip can be replaced with a fusible red clay or perhaps an estuarine mud. A tri-axial blend of a local red clay with whiting and China clay or ball clay should provide similar

results. This glaze is basically one with a high calcia content and will provide the sort of textured, runny effects that might be expected from certain high ash content glazes. Robert Tichane suggests the following recipe:

Albany slip	64
China clay	16
Whiting	20

but this should be regarded as no more than a starting point for your own experimentation.

All the glazes are sprayed for greater control of thickness of application. Tom also often uses a system of wax resist or one that requires self-adhesive paper stickers. The areas of resist are then highlighted with trailed dots of white and green glaze. The 'kinetic' decoration is nothing more than a suggestion on Tom's part. The judicious use of the resist and the careful placing of one, more fluid, glaze over another simply begs the pot and the kiln to do their best work on the potter's behalf.

Tom Turner's pots are sharp and precise in form yet soft and mellow in their surface quality. He is a superlative technician both in the making of his forms and the glazes that cover them. Tom's historical references include the Chinese Song and Tang dynasties and also the American stonewares of the 18th and early 19th centuries (example on page 17). Talking of his work he says, 'My work grows very slowly over a long period of time through trial and error, new directions come out of the work itself, today suggests tomorrow'.

He will name a number of craftsmen, not all potters, who are admired, because to him they 'exemplify the magnificence of craft'. Tom Turner's pots are certainly magnificent examples of the potter's craft.

* Veegum T is a magnesium alumina silicate that is much more plastic than bentonite but not commercially available in the UK.

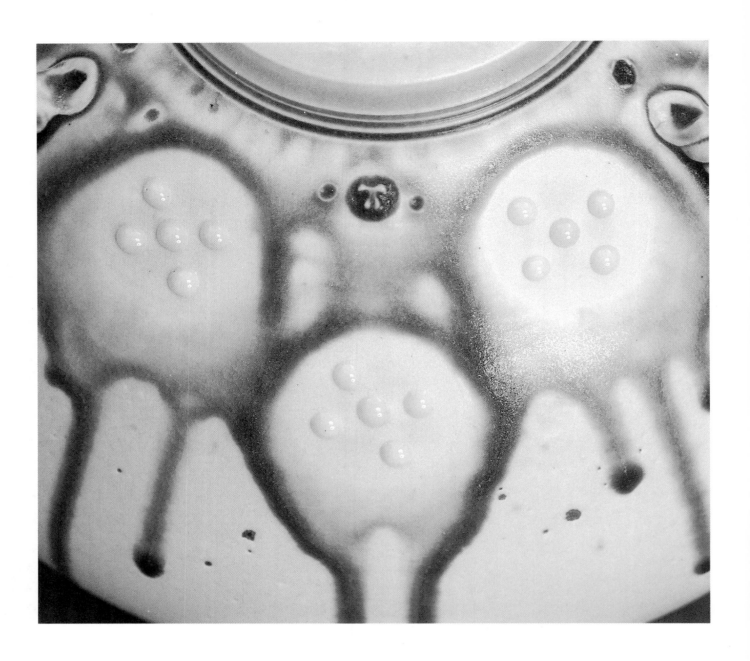

Page 126

Lidded jar, 9" high.

On this jar can be seen the sort of glaze thickness control that can be achieved by spraying on the glaze. The thicker, runnier area at the top of the pot is the same glaze as the rest of the jar except it is thicker and has been fluxed a little more by the addition of iron oxide between the circles of dotted decoration. The circular areas are bare porcelain body and were achieved by the use of sticky paper labels. The glaze is the 'ash like' glaze mentioned in the text.

Page 127

Tom calls this pot a 'Spouted Vessel'. It has been glazed by exactly the same process. On this example the 'kinetic' nature of the high lime glaze can be seen to great effect. The bare patch circles direct the flow of glaze in such a way as to capture the essence of melted, flowing glass at the same time creating a real feeling of movement over the surface of the pot.

Page 128
Close up of jar on page 130

Top page 130

A lidded jar, 11" high.

Made in two pieces and joined while leather hard just prior to the turning stage. The glaze is a combination of two-thirds of the Leach 4.4.2. using oak ash and one-third of the 'ash like' high lime glaze with an addition of 2% of iron oxide. The brown crystalline area over the shoulder of the pot develops as a result of a thicker glaze coating in that area. You may like to try combining glazes in this manner. It can be done by simply adding quantities of one slop to another or by carefully working out mathematically the proportions of materials required by the use of the appropriate recipes.

Bottom page 130

A rounded bottle vase, $7\frac{1}{2}$" high.

The whole of this pot was sprayed with the 4.4.2. mixture mentioned earlier. In this case the ash is a mixture of hardwoods from Tom's wood-burning stove. He says that he prefers apple ash but can't always get it. There is an iron oxide wash over the areas that have turned yellow to brown.

Page 131

A large lidded jar, 19" high.

This is a very large pot by any standard. The fact that it's made in porcelain makes it all the more remarkable. Again, it was made in two sections and later joined. It has Tom's green assimilated ash glaze sprayed on thinly before a wax resist and a subsequent second coating of the same glaze. Can you see what I meant, when I mentioned in the text, about the clean, crisp lines of Tom's work combined with the soft, misty flowing surfaces?

Right
Lidded jar

Below
Vase

Opposite
Jar

Other Potters
who use Ash Glazes

Bottle by Patrick Sargent, 9" high.

Patrick Sargent was born in Northampton in 1956, was trained at West Surrey College of Art in Farnham, England and has now set up his workshop in Switzerland. His pots are fired in an Anagama-style kiln and rely in large measure on the accidental effects of fly ash at high temperatures for their decoration.

In the main this book deals with glazes that contain wood ash which are then applied to the pot prior to placing in the kiln. This photograph shows how a 'glaze' can occur without prior application merely as a result of the build up over a long firing cycle of a deposit of 'fly ash' on the pot which combines with the silica in the clay to form a glass.

Patrick Sargent fires his 172 cu. ft. kiln for almost two days. This, combined with a frequent raking of the embers which sends large clouds of ash into the chamber along with vaporised fluxes of potash and soda, creates the wonderfully rich surfaces on the carefully and strategically placed pots.

Bottom left page 134

Small jampot with an incised decoration by Ursula Mommens

Ursula Mommens has her pottery in Sussex, England. She began potting under the guidance of Dora Billington and William Straite Murray and then later joined Michael Cardew at Wenford Bridge

Apple ash glaze of:

Apple ash	44
Feldspar	44
China clay	12

Reduction begins at 800°C and is heavy for one hour and then more moderate until 1280°C. Ursula wood fires for 17 hours.

Top left page 134

Two wood-fired stoneware bottles. Tallest Ht. 9".

John Leach has his workshop at Muchelney in Somerset where he works with two assistants to produce a range of wood-fired stoneware, kitchen and tableware along with a number of more individual pieces of a more idiosyncratic nature. His training as a potter began with a five-year apprenticeship to his father, David, followed by periods with Ray Finch at Winchcombe and Colin Pearson and then three years with his grandfather, Bernard Leach.

Neither of the two bottles shown here have an ash 'glaze' in the true sense of the word. The handled flask on the right shows the effect of the woodfire while the other has a less toasted colour but they both illustrate another technique involving wood ash. John often dusts pure wood ash from a muslin bag over the tops of the pots just as they are put into the kiln. This ash then melts and combines with a little alumina from the pots' surface to form a partial glaze to run downwards in rivulets thus emphasising the form of the pot.

Right page 134

A tall slender bottle by David Leach. 18" high.

David Leach began potting in 1930 with his father, Bernard, at St. Ives and continued as his father's 'right arm' until beginning his own workshop at Bovey Tracey in Devon in 1955. Since then he has earned an international reputation for his stoneware and porcelain all over the world and at the time of writing is celebrating 60 years as a potter.

Not all ash glazes have ash as the major flux. Often ash is added to a glaze as a modifier. It may lend a softness to the fired glaze because of its complex nature that further additions of, for instance, whiting may not provide. The glaze on this bottle is an Old Leach Pottery standard. In this case the bottle has been dipped in an iron slip of 75% ball clay and 25% red iron oxide and the pattern drawn through the wet glaze with a combed tool. The glaze was then dipped over the slip.

Recipe.		
	Talc	5
	Ball clay	23
	China clay	5
	Whiting	2.5
	Hardwood ash	12.5
	Cornish stone	52

Left page 135

Teapot. 9½" high by Terry Bell-Hughes.

Terry Bell-Hughes says of his work, 'The pots are thrown, sometimes slipped with red or white slip, brushed or combed or finger wiped, others are left plain. The work is then bisque fired to 1000°C and then dipped in ash or feldspathic glazes. Wood ash is often used raw over the other glazes. The glaze firing is at 1280°C in a reducing atmosphere. The best pots that emerge after the firing are those that seem to have left "me", as the maker, behind.'

The marks of the combed slip are clearly visible on this elongated, rather eccentric teapot and the darker colour of the body clay is showing through. The slashes of cobalt blue have been added with bold sweeps of a brush on top of the glaze which is a pale green celadon for which the recipe is:

Mixed ash	30
Potash feldspar	20
China clay	5
Ball clay	5

Left page 135

A Round Bottomed Dish with two Handles. 13½" diameter.

Takeshi Yasuda spent his formative years as a potter at Mashiko, the pottery village in his native Japan that had been the home of Hamada. He came to work in the UK in 1973 and settled in Devon where he now works with his wife, potter Sandy Brown.

Until 1978 Takeshi's glazes had been ash based but a visit to Norway changed his approach. As he says, 'I could not get any ash in Norway. So I made my first non-ash ash glaze. It worked first time. It was quite miraculously exactly like my real ash glaze. It was so good that I still use this first recipe.'

Takeshi has taken a mixed ash analysis from a book and reconstructed his glaze using the substitute instead of his ash. Now that much of his work is oxidised he still retains the same formula with some minor adjustments depending on the fire.

Clay body	Ball clay (Hy-plas 71)	90	
	Grog 30–85	5	
	60–Dust	5	
	Red iron oxide	1	for oxidation
		0.5	for reduction
Slip	Ball clay (Hy-plas 71)	10	
	China clay (W.B.B. No 50)	4	
	Zirconium silicate	1	
Glaze	Potash feldspar (FFF)	20	
	Nephaline syenite	15	
	Whiting	20	
	Talc	10	
	China clay	15	
	Quartz	15	
	Bone ash	2	
	Manganese dioxide	0.15	for oxidation firing
		0.3	for reduction firing
	Synthetic red iron oxide	0.8	for oxidation firing
		1.5	for reduction firing

Top right page 135

A tall, slender pitcher by Bernard Leach, 12" high.

I believe that had it not been for Bernard Leach most of us who are potters today would be something else. Indeed, through his writing, teaching and magnificent example, he was largely responsible for the Western, 20th-century craft revival in its broadest sense. Few people, in any field, have had such influence upon their contemporaries, seeing the roots of their belief spread so deeply and so widely in their own lifetime.

This pitcher was made toward the end of Bernard's potting career when his eyesight was beginning to fail him. Yet it displays a complete rightness of form. Its relaxed and gentle curves punctuated by a firm, definite rim create a strength reminiscent of its medieval predecessors.

The glaze is probably a mixture of wood ash and clay in roughly equal proportions. By the colour of the glaze, it would seem that the clay contained some iron, possibly a local red clay such as that from St Erth or maybe Fremington. In *A Potter's Book*, Bernard mentions that he had produced glazes remarkably similar to some early Chinese glazes, as this is, by combining a siliceous buff clay with 40% of oak ash.

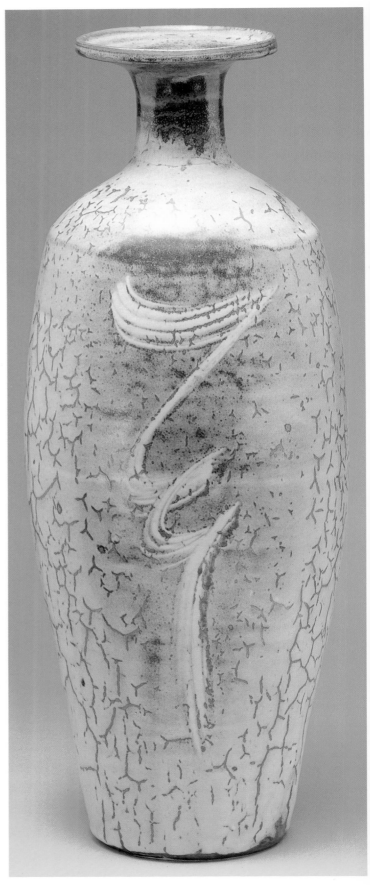

Top left
Two bottles

Bottom left
Jampot

Right
Tall vase

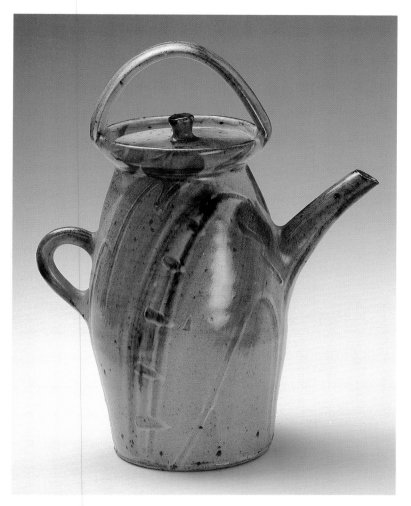

Top left
Teapot

Top right
Pitcher

Left
Round bottomed dish

Ash Glaze Recipes

The following recipes are intended as the basis for your own experiments although it is a fact that, because of the variability of wood ash as a glaze material, your equivalents of these recipes will rarely be exactly the same as the originals. Don't let this worry you. The 'difference' in your glaze will be the individual character that your ash or local material imparts for you.

Remember what I told you in the text of the book, that your ash glaze may need adjustment before it fires the way that the recipe suggests that it should. Other potters may have a different method of preparing the ash or they may not wash their ash at all. Try the recipes, alter them, substitute one material for another, play around with the percentages. In short, use the recipes as a creative tool ever mindful of your eventual goal, the creation of glazes that are yours and no one else's.

1 *1280°C Reduction*

Any ash	53
Cornish stone	14.5
Potash feldspar	14.5
China clay	6.5
Whiting	4.5
Quartz	7

This is my standard and most used glaze. It forms the basic formula and is used with many different ashes. The last three ingredients may need to be altered depending on the ash.

2

Ash	47
China clay	8
Feldspar	21
Whiting	8
Quartz	9
Dolomite	7

A similar glaze to **1** but usually lighter in tone.

3 *1280°C Reduction*

Ash	50
Feldspar	21.5
China clay	7
Whiting	3.5
Quartz	18

4 *From Katherine Pleydell-Bouverie*

Petalite	6
Soda feldspar	28
China clay	7
Quartz	10
Ash	31
Whiting	17

A pale green.

5 *Another from Katherine Pleydell-Bouverie*
1280°C Reduction

Grass ash	33
China clay	15
Feldspar	44
Calcium borate frit	7

This glaze I also use in the salt kiln. It fires a smooth Shino-like surface with a tea leaf crystal pattern.

6 *From Alan Brunsden*

1280°C Reduction

Potash feldspar	30
Mixed wood ash	43
Ball clay	17
Talc	8
Quartz	8
Bentonite	2

Ash washed three times. Heavy reduction from 1000°C for green breaking to brown. Also suitable for oxidation.

7 *From Jim Malone*

Shap hornfels	25
Shap pink granite	75
Hawthorn ash	100
Ball clay	50

This is a variation of the classic 40.40.20 formula where Jim Malone has used materials local to him. Try substituting your own local stone dusts or feldspar with a small addition of iron.

8 *From Warren MacKenzie*

1280°C Reduction

4 parts ash
5 parts fusible red clay (Albany slip)

A great many different effects depending on the thickness of application and firing temperature. Try using a local clay or an estuarine mud. Nigel Wood, in his book *Oriental Glazes*, passes on a formula that should provide a good synthetic Albany slip.

9 *1280–1300°C Reduction* but will also work in oxidation at the upper temperature limits.

Feldspar	60
Ash	50
Quartz	40

This is the basic recipe that simulates the Japanese Nuka glaze which is made from rice husk ash. It is an opaque opalescent glaze with a blue, chun-like quality. I have altered this glaze to a pale cream by substituting half the feldspar with the same amount of iron-bearing granite.

10 *From Muriel Harris*

For Oxidation to 1230–1250°C

Seaweed ash	38
Feldspar	36
China clay	8
Ball clay	8
Flint	10

11 *From Walter Keeler*

i)	Feldspar	45.6
	China clay	4.5
	Ash	13.6
	Whiting	9.5
	Yellow ochre	27.6

This glaze is also suitable for the salt kiln. The type and quality of the ochre profoundly affects the result.

A storejar by Walter Keeler, 8" high.
The glaze on the upper half of this jar is:

Ash	4
Potash feldspar	2
Red clay	1

The red clay is local to Walter Keeler in the Monmouth area of Wales but similar results can be obtained from various 'local' red clays. The iron content of the clay should not be too high or a very dark glaze should be expected. (See the line blend of ash and red clay in colour test 5, p. 63.)
Author's Collection

ii) Red clay   60
    Unwashed ash   20
    Nephaline syenite 20

iii) Ash   4
     Feldspar   2
     Red clay   1

Both of these last two can be used for raw glazing, the first at leather hard and the second at bone dry.

12 Ash   50
    China clay   50

This is a dry, stony matte that can be used both in oxidation and reduction at 1280°C. Different thicknesses will provide varying colours. Excellent response to added oxides especially cobalt/copper mixes.

13 *For Oxidation. 1270–1280°C*
    Elm ash   80
    Potash feldspar 40
    Whiting   40
    Ball clay   70

A smooth light grey turning to mottled gold where thicker. Apply over a smooth low iron body.

14 *For Oxidation. 1280°C*
    Ash   50
    Red clay   50

Depending on the red clay, an Indian red breaking to an ochre mottle where thicker.

15 *For Oxidation. 1280°C*
    Ash   30
    Feldspar   30
    Ball clay 20
    Whiting   10
    Red clay   10

15a *For Oxidation*
    Ash   40
    Feldspar   40
    Any clay   20
    + additions of 10%
    dolomite, talc etc.

An excellent glaze for domestic ware. A blue/grey colour.

16 *From Philip Revell*
    i) *Reconstructed ash celadon. 1280°C Reduction*
       Potash feldspar 19
       Whiting   31
       Talc   2.4
       Bone ash   2.4
       Ball clay   6
       Quartz   9
       Cornish stone   15
       China clay   15
       Red iron oxide   1

    ii) *Reconstructed 'Nuka' glaze*
        Potash feldspar   36
        Whiting   22
        Talc   2
        Bone ash   2
        Ball clay   6
        Quartz   30
        Boro-calcite frit 3

17 *From Ray Finch*
    1280–1300°C Reduction

    Ash   30
    Feldspar   55
    China clay   10
    Flint   5
    Black iron oxide 1

18 *From Tom and Ginny Marsh*
    Cone 9. Matt
    i) Ash   40
       Custer (potash)   40
       feldspar
       Georgia kaolin   20

    ii) Local earthenware 50
        clay
        Hardwood ash   50

A tall, faceted bottle from Mashiko, Japan. 14" high.
There is a quality to this bottle that gives the impression that it may have been hewn from solid rock. The faceting has been done quickly with complete confidence and the ragged cut marks at the base are totally at one with the overall feel of the pot. Sadly, this wonderful expression of the joy in working with clay and glaze is so often lacking in much Western studio pottery of recent years.
    The glaze is 'Nuka' over which a tenmoku has been trailed loosely from a full brush. Despite its rather solid appearance, I have handled this pot and I can vouch for its 'physical' lightness.

Ash Analyses

	SiO$_2$	Al$_2$O$_3$	Fe$_2$O$_3$	TiO$_2$	CaO	MgO	K$_2$O	Na$_2$O	MnO	P$_2$O$_5$
Apple wood	1.31	—	1.66	—	63.6	7.46	19.24	10.45	—	4.9
Beech	5.45	—	1.0	—	55.5	10.9	16.5	4.0	—	5.45
Birch	3.84	—	1.0	—	57.5	7.69	12.53	7.69	—	7.69
Oak, English	15.3	.13	2.4	—	30.02	12.01	14.00	9.12	.1	13.8
Oak, China	39.81	15.11	3.58	—	23.54	4.09	5.77	1.47	4.32	2.3
Oak, Japan	39.62	16.34	3.83	—	23.69	4.14	5.68	1.52	1.01	2.62
Pine	24.39	9.71	3.41	—	39.73	4.45	8.98	3.77	2.74	4.45
Willow	4.44	.05	1.25	—	20.21	8.26	49.8	2.5	.18	10.0
Rice husk	94.36	1.78	.61	—	1.04	—	1.35		—	—
Wheat straw	67.5	—	.6	—	5.8	2.5	13.6	1.4	—	4.8
Fern	55.02	19.32	1.67	.3	8.59	7.44	4.81	.56	1.36	.92
Lawn grass	39.64	16.60	3.44	—	12.88	5.65	6.19	6.20	—	9.0
Meadow hay	29.57	—	1.0	—	11.56	5.0	25.67	7.0	—	6.2

Molecular Weights

A list of molecular weights for some of the oxides and materials most commonly used in reconstructing ash substitutes.

Name	Chemical formula	MW
Alumina	Al$_2$O$_3$	102.0
Bone ash	Ca$_3$(PO$_4$)$_2$	310.3
Calcia	CaO	56.1
Calcium carbonate	CaCO$_3$	100.1
China clay	Al$_2$O$_3$ 2SiO$_2$ 2H$_2$O	258.2
Dolomite	CaMg(CO$_3$)$_2$	184.4
Potash feldspar	K$_2$O Al$_2$O$_3$ 6SiO$_2$	556.8
Soda feldspar	Na$_2$O Al$_2$O$_3$ 6SiO$_2$	524.6
Ferric oxide (red iron)	Fe$_2$O$_3$	159.6
Flint	SiO$_2$	60.1
Iron oxide (black)	FeO	71.8
Limestone	CaCO$_3$	100.1
Magnesia	MgO	40.3
Magnesium carbonate	MgCO$_3$	84.3
Manganese dioxide	MnO$_2$	86.9
Manganous oxide	MnO	70.9
Nepheline syenite	K$_2$O 3Na$_2$O 4Al$_2$O$_3$ 9SiO$_2$	1169.0
Phosphorus pentoxide	P$_2$O$_5$	142.0
Potash	K$_2$O	94.2
Potassium carbonate	K$_2$CO$_3$	138.2
Quartz	SiO$_2$	60.1
Soda	Na$_2$O	62.0
Soda ash	Na$_2$O$_3$	106.0
Talc	3MgO 4SiO$_2$ H$_2$O	379.3
Whiting	CaCO$_3$	100.1
Wollastonite	CaSiO$_3$	116.2

Glossary

Alkali
The opposite of an acid. Potters call their glaze and body fluxes their alkalis. Soda, potash, magnesia and calcia are all alkaline substances that have a fluxing action on silica at high temperatures. They all occur in wood and vegetable ashes.

Amphoteric
A substance capable of acting as either acid or alkali in a glaze. The amphoteric substances are important in glaze making as they act as a link between the acidic glass formers and the alkaline fluxes. In this role they are known as stabilisers and alumina is the most important amphoteric oxide as far as the potter is concerned.

Ash
The grey or pink powdery substance that is the inorganic residue left after the burning of animal or vegetable matter. A source of body and glaze fluxes for the potter.

Ash Glaze
In my terms, any glaze that contains wood or plant ash in any amount. Some potters would argue that ash must be the main or only flux for a glaze to qualify as an ash glaze.

Ball Mill
Sometimes called a pebble mill. A cylindrical drum into which is placed material that one wishes to reduce in particle size. Along with the material to be ground some water and pebbles, usually flint or bisqued porcelain, are added and the tumbling action continuously crushes the material into even smaller particle size.

Basalt
An igneous rock with a high iron content that will melt around 1250°C. Useful glaze base.

Base
Another term for alkali.

Batch
A specific weight of materials that will provide a specific quantity of glaze slop.

Blistering
A sharp crater in the surface of the glaze left by escaping gas while the glaze was molten.

Bone Ash
Calcined animal bones that have been finely ground for use in bodies and glazes. A source of both calcia and phosphorus pentoxide and therefore useful in the reconstruction of specific wood ashes.

Calcine
To heat a substance to a high temperature so as to remove water or combustible material. Ash is sometimes calcined to remove carbonaceous matter.

Celadon
A general name for any pale blue or green glaze coloured by the reduction firing of iron oxide.

Chun
A pale blue opalescent stoneware glaze. The opalescence is due to the phosphate content of the glaze which is usually derived from plant or bone ash.

Crazing
A glaze defect, or attractive feature depending on your point of view, characterised by a network of fine cracks.

Devitrification
The crystallization of a glaze upon cooling. A fast cooling cycle will often cause a normally frosted glaze to be clear and glassy.

Eutectic

The eutectic point is that optimum mixture of two or more materials that will melt at the lowest possible temperature. (See pp. 48–50.)

Feldspar

A generic term for a group of minerals that contain all the oxides necessary to create stoneware glazes within themselves i.e. silica, alumina and an alkali. They are sometimes referred to as 'potter's gold' and can be regarded as natural frits.

Flint

SiO_2. An almost pure form of silica.

Flux

A glaze ingredient that promotes ceramic fusion by its action on other oxides (most often silica) within the glaze.

Frit

If a glaze material is troublesome in some way, it could be soluble or poisonous, or if a special colour requirement is desired, then it can be melted either alone or in combination with other materials to form a glass. It is then re-ground to a fine powder and added to a glaze in the usual way.

Glaze

The layer of glass that is fused to the surface of a piece of pottery for practical and aesthetic purposes.

Glaze-Body Layer

That area of interaction where glaze meets clay body.

Grain Size

Particle size. Materials with a fine grain size will dissolve into the glaze melt earlier than the same material with a larger grain size.

Granite

An igneous rock rich in silica and alumina with a variable iron content. Useful as a glaze material. It can be regarded as feldspar for the purposes of experiment.

Kaki

A glaze named after the Japanese persimmon fruit, the colour of which it resembles. The rich, red rust colour is due to iron oxide crystals on the surface of the glaze.

Lime

Calcia (calcium oxide, CaO). The alkaline oxide used as a flux in glazes. It is introduced into glazes as limestone or whiting which are both calcium carbonate. On heating the carbonate decomposes to give calcia and carbon dioxide.

Limestone

Calcium carbonate ($CaCO_3$). Potters' whiting is often crushed limestone.

Magnesia

Magnesium oxide (MgO). A high temperature glaze flux present in most wood ashes.

Manganous Oxide

A metal oxide used as a colourant for bodies and glazes. TOXIC.

Ochre

A naturally occurring fine clay with a high iron content. Useful as a slip covering that will colour the glaze coat.

Organic Matter

That portion of any living organism that has a carbon basis. Carbon does not melt but oxidises to become a gas.

Oxidation Firing

To fire a kiln with an ample supply of oxygen. The opposite is a reduction firing.

Pearl Ash

Potassium carbonate. (K_2CO_3).

Phosphorus Pentoxide

(P_2O_5) A glass-forming oxide responsible for the chun effect and introduced into glazes via plant and bone ashes.

Potash

Potassium oxide (K_2O). An alkaline flux.

Proto-Porcelain

In simple terms a collective name for early Chinese stonewares, often ash-glazed, that were the forerunners of true stonewares and porcelain.

Quartz

(SiO_2) Pure silica. A hazardous dust.

R-Groups

For simplicity and easier understanding of the chemistry of glazes the oxides used in glaze making are separated into three groups. Within these groups the chemical symbols for the element is substituted by the letter R. Group 1 is the RO group and contains all the bases or alkaline fluxes, e.g. CaO. Group 2 is the R_2O_3 group and called the amphoteric oxides. Oxides in this group can also play partial roles in groups 1 and 3, e.g. potash feldspar R_2O R_2O_3 $6RO_2$. Group 3 is the RO_2 group and are acidic. They are glass formers of which silica is the most important.

Reduction

The action of taking oxygen away from the metal oxides.

Reduction Firing

To carry out a kiln firing whilst restricting the amount of oxygen available to the wares.

Salt Glaze
The reaction of soda with silica and alumina. The soda is derived from common salt introduced into the kiln during the firing.

Shivering
A glaze defect where thin, sharp slivers of glaze part company with the pot. It is a result of poor glaze fit and usually happens on the rims of pots or edges of handles. It is the opposite effect to crazing.

Sieve
A mesh stretched across a frame used for the separation of particles above a certain size from the main bulk of the material. A 60's and an 80's mesh serve most of my purposes but one would need a 100's or 120's for finer glazes; celadons for instance require a greater distribution of materials.

Silica
Silicon dioxide (SiO_2). The main glass-forming oxide for glazes. An element of fundamental importance to potters.

Soda
Sodium oxide (Na_2O). One of the three strong alkaline oxides used as fluxes in glazes.

Soda Ash
Sodium carbonate (Na_2CO_3). At one time soda ash referred to the ashes of burnt sea plants.

Tenmoku
Popularly, the name given to any dark brown or black stoneware glaze stained with iron. Their origins can be traced back to the early black glazed wares of the Qi Dynasty 600 BC.

Unomi
The correct name for the Japanese teabowl.

Water-Smoking
The initial stages of a bisque fire as the atmospherically held water is driven off. This process must be taken very slowly to avoid shattering the pots.

Whiting
In potters' terms, calcium carbonate (q.v.).

Wicket
The removable brick 'door' to the kiln.

Small box by Richard Batterham, $4\frac{1}{2}$" across.
The fluid ash glaze has highlighted the decoration beautifully on this thrown box. Note how the turning of the lid has allowed for the glaze to pool at the outer edge.
Author's collection.

Bibliography

Cardew, Michael, *Pioneer Pottery* (Longman, 1969)

Crafts Council, *Katherine Pleydell-Bouverie, a Potter's Life 1895–1985* (Crafts Council, 1985)

Gompertz, G. St. G.M., *Celadon Wares* (Faber & Faber, 1968)

Hamer, Frank & Janet, *The Potter's Dictionary of Materials and Techniques* (A & C Black, 1975)

Hopper, Robin, *The Ceramic Spectrum* (Collins, 1984)

Leach, Bernard, *Hamada, Potter* (Kodansha, 1975)

Leach, Bernard, *A Potter's Book* (Faber & Faber, 1940)

Mason, Ralph, *Native Clays and Glazes for North American Potters* (Timber Press, 1981)

Peterson, Susan, *Shoji Hamada, A Potter's Way and Work* (Kodansha, 1974)

Rhodes, Daniel, *Clay and Glazes for the Potter* (A & C Black; Chilton, 1957)

Sato, Masahiko, *Chinese Ceramics, a Short History* (Weatherhill, 1978)

Sinnott, Edmund, *Botany, Principals and Problems* (McGraw-Hill, 1935)

Sutherland, Brian, *Glazes from Natural Sources* (Batsford, 1987)

Tichane, Robert, *Ash Glazes* (New York State Institute for Glaze Research, 1987)

Wolff, Dr. Emil, *Aschen-Analysen* (Verlag von Wiegandt & Hempel, 1871)

Wood, Nigel, *Iron in the Fire* (Oriental Ceramic Society, 1988)

Wood, Nigel, *Oriental Glazes* (A & C Black, 1978)

The *Ceramic Review*, published by the Craftsmen Potters Association of Great Britain often has articles related to ash glazes and is generally an ongoing fund of ceramic knowledge as is *Ceramics Monthly* in the USA.

Index